When Violence
Is No Stranger

When Violence Is No Stranger

Pastoral Counseling with Survivors of Acquaintance Rape

Kristen J. Leslie

Fortress Press
Minneapolis

Cover art: *Portrait in Orange* by Diana Ong © Diana Ong/SuperStock. Used by permission. • Cover design: Marti Naughton • Interior design: Beth Wright

Acknowledgment is made for permission to quote from *For Colored Girls Who Have Considered Suicide/When the Rainbow Is Enuf* by Ntozake Shange. Copyright ©1975, Collier Books, New York. Used by permission of Simon and Schuster.

A portion of this book has appeared as "When Violence Is No Stranger: Pastoral Care and Acquaintance Rape, " *Journal of Religion and Abuse* vol. 3 (3/4), 2001: 113–42, and is used by permission of the Haworth Pastoral Press, Binghamton, New York.

Scripture quotations, unless otherwise noted, are from the New Revised Standard Version (NRSV) Bible, copyright © 1989 by the Division of Christian Education of the National Council of the Churches of Christ in the USA, and are used by permission.

Scripture quotations from the Revised Standard Version (RSV) of the Bible are copyright © 1946, 1952, 1971 by the Division of Christian Education of the National Council of the Churches of Christ in the USA, and are used by permission.

Library of Congress Cataloging-in-Publication Data

Leslie, Kristen Jane.
   When violence is no stranger : pastoral counseling with survivors of acquaintance rape / Kristen J. Leslie.
       p. cm.
Includes bibliographical references and index.
   ISBN 0-8006-3575-2 (pbk. : alk. paper)
   1. Acquaintance rape victims—Pastoral counseling of. 2. Abused women—Pastoral counseling of. I. Title.
BV4445.5.L47 2002
259'.086'949--dc21

                    2002152637

The paper used in this publication meets the minimum requirements of American National Standard for Information Sciences — Permanence of Paper for Printed Library Materials, ANSI Z329.48-1984.

Manufactured in the U.S.A.
07   06   05   04   03   1   2   3   4   5   6   7   8   9   10

To my parents, Betty and Jim,
for whom justice is an everyday thing

Contents

. . . but if you've been seen in public wit him
danced one dance
kissed him good-bye lightly

wit closed mouth

pressin charges will be as hard
as keeping yr legs closed
while five fools try to run a train on you

these men friends of ours
who smile nice . . .

we must have known

women relinquish all personal rights
in the presence of a man
who apparently cd be considered a rapist

especially if he has been considered a friend

& is no less worthy of bein beat within an inch of his life
being publicly ridiculed
havin two fists shoved up his ass

than the stranger
we always thot it wd be

who never showed up

cuz it turns out the nature of rape has changed

we can now meet them in circles we frequent for companionship
we see them at the coffeehouse
wit someone else we know
we cd even have em over for dinner
& get raped in our own houses
by invitation
a friend. . . .

—Ntozake Shange, *for colored girls who have considered suicide /*
when the rainbow is enuf

Preface

Reading about rape is hard to do. It requires that you face the suffering caused by an unthinkable act: violence by a friend. Friends aren't supposed to hurt friends; they certainly aren't supposed to rape them. But they do. And when it happens, a woman's world is shattered. This book is about how violence by an acquaintance can shatter a woman's world and how, with the help of friends, families, faith communities, and pastoral caregivers, she can heal.

Recently a colleague asked me if this was a hard book to write. It was. It was hard on my sense of safety in the world, and it was hard on my relationships with men. Although this book is about rape, I did not write it so that I could learn about rape itself; I no more want to stand in the face of evil than anyone does. I wrote about rape because there is life after rape. Women who have been raped somehow find the courage to wake in the morning, put their feet on the ground, and make it through the day. In these stories of survival there is hope. That is why I wrote this book, and I believe that is why you are reading it. If you are a pastoral caregiver or other interested professional, this work will inform you of the unique needs of the acquaintance rape survivor, enable you to accompany her in the long task of rebuilding her world, and make a difference in how accessible and how safe you are to her. If you are a caring friend or family member of a survivor, learning about the effects of rape can help you understand her lonely experience and how you might help. If you are a survivor of acquaintance rape or another form of sexualized violence, I pray this book offers you the voice and hope you seek. Reading and speaking the words can make a difference.

I started thinking about acquaintance rape when I was a college chaplain some fifteen years ago. It started because a woman who had been raped found her way to my office. Word got out that I was willing to listen and believe, and more women came. With no formal training in issues of sexualized violence, I found myself scrambling for any workshop or lecture that would help equip me to understand these women's sufferings. This became my pursuit in graduate school. As a part of my pastoral counseling clinical training I participated in an Office of Criminal Justice Planning rape crisis training sponsored by the gifted and committed staff of Project SISTER, a rape crisis and prevention agency in Pomona, California. As a rape crisis advocate and counselor I worked with staff and clients who taught me what it meant to stand with courage in the face of evil. I am grateful to Theresa Borunda, Carolyn Dominguez, Evelyn Stone, Mary Richey, and other members of the Project SISTER community for their lifelong commitments to the healing work of sexual assault crisis and prevention.

I was able to think and write about violence and healing because many people helped. I am grateful to all the women who have shared their stories with me. Your stories make a healing difference to other survivors and to those of us who want to help. An amazing circle of friends has sustained me through this long process. My loving thanks goes to Elaine Balsley, Doug Brown, Sue Asher, Serene Jones, JoClare Wilson, Nancy McCormack, Letty Russell, Shannon Clarkson, Yolanda Smith, Marit Trelstad, Cynthia Terry, and Mimi Walters. At a point where I began to doubt my own sense of things, Michael West at Fortress Press enthusiastically adopted this book, and so to him I say thanks. I am grateful to Kaudie McLean, Mandy Brummer, and Lisa Jeffcoat McNeal for their editorial and research support, as well as the Wabash Center for Teaching and Learning, which provided financial and communal support as I edited this work. And finally, from the beginning my spouse, Michael Boddy, has been close at hand, offering unconditional support and a firm belief in this work. Thank you, love.

1.

Introduction

It is not enemies who taunt me—
  I could bear that;
it is not adversaries who deal insolently with me—
  I could hide from them.
But it is you, my equal, my companion, my familiar friend,
with whom I kept pleasant company;
we walked in the house of God with the throng.
                                        —Ps. 55:12-14

Since the day Sophie walked into my office, I have been concerned about how survivors heal from the trauma of acquaintance rape. Sophie's story is not unusual. She had been to a party where she had a few beers. When she announced she was heading home, David volunteered to escort her. At her room, David forced his way in and raped Sophie. She told only a few close friends; she did not tell her family. She thought she could "stuff it away." Two years passed, and something came up in class that brought it all back. She could not eat, she could not sleep, she could not be in crowds, and she could not make sense of what was happening to her. Sophie walked into my office asking for help.

I was the college chaplain, and I knew little about acquaintance rape. As a girl, I had been reared to be wary of dark alleys and unfamiliar men in trench coats. I was taught that as long as women locked their doors, moved en masse (never alone), had well-lighted sidewalks, and dressed appropriately, the dangers were minimal. But Sophie's experience of violence did not fit into these categories. Rape by a friend: That seemed to me a contradiction in terms. If I were experiencing such cognitive dissonance, I could only imagine the confusion Sophie must have been experiencing. I needed to know more if I were going to be of any help to Sophie. I also knew that if I needed to know the facts, so, too, did other religious professionals and pastoral caregivers.

Clergy and other religious professionals are in a good position for helping survivors of acquaintance rape. Polls have shown that a majority of people seeking help for mental heath issues prefer (1) to turn to professionals who present spiritual values and beliefs and (2) to have their own values and beliefs integrated into the helping process.[1] Because people look to clergy and religious professionals as important sources of comfort and support, these representatives of faith communities are in a crucial position to help those who suffer from traumas, such as acquaintance rape. It does not mean, however, that these professionals have the necessary training to help. Religious professionals have a range of experiences with survivors of acquaintance rape. Some seek out extensive training. Many, however, are ill-equipped to be pastorally effective. To be caring partners in the healing process, religious professionals must (1) know the prevalence and definitions of acquaintance rape as discussed above; (2) know the facts and distortions about acquaintance rape, including why some women do not report and the consequences if they do; (3) understand some theoretical constructions relating to brokenness and healing, including sociohistorical, trauma, and pastoral theological theories; (4) appropriately respond to a survivor's needs while being aware of sensitive issues surrounding these responses; and (5) make informed and appropriate referrals. We will attend to these latter four tasks in the following chapters.

Prevalence of Acquaintance Rape

Acquaintance rape is not an aberration. It is an everyday part of a young adult woman's "education." It is, Judith Herman suggests, a societal initiation into the coercive violence of adult society.[2] Statistics tell us the startling truth: For American women over age 18,

- 1 in 3 are sexually assaulted in their life times,
- 1.3 are raped every minute,
- 78 per hour,
- 1871 per day,
- 683,000 per year.[3]

One in four or five women (20 to 25 percent) on a college campus is the survivor of rape or attempted rape, and the overwhelming majority (84 percent) of those rapes or attempted rapes are committed by an acquaintance.[4] One in five rapes (22 percent) is committed against women ages eighteen to twenty-four.[5] Tersely put, the majority of rapes are not committed by the stranger from the bushes, but by the family member, friend, or colleague from next door. Fear of the unknown thus yields to fear of the known, the familiar, the trusted.

But the trauma does not end there. Because women experience fear (brought on by real and perceived threats), guilt, shame, self-blame, and distrust of authority systems, less than 16 percent of survivors of acquaintance rape report their assaults to law enforcement agencies. The number is even lower for African American women.[6] Further, the same number of individuals who do not report the rape to authorities (84 percent) do not seek medical assistance following the acquaintance rape.[7] Too often, rape survivors feel they are victimized by medical personnel.

So What Is Acquaintance Rape?

Legally, acquaintance rape is an event that occurs without the victim's consent, involving the use or threat of force to penetrate the victim's vagina or anus by penis, tongue, finger(s), or object, or the victim's mouth by penis. This action occurs between an adult victim and one or more adult assailants who know each other.[8] Such invasive penetration can be obtained by physical force, by threat of bodily harm, or when the victim is incapable of giving consent by virtue of mental illness, mental retardation, or intoxication.[9] Forced, nonconsensual sexual activity is a crime. The relationship between the woman and the perpetrator before the rape can be as friend, classmate, lover, former lover, coworker, employee–employer, clergy–parishioner, or known passer-by. Such sexualized violence can happen in relationships, even close ones, that have no prior sexual component. "Date rape," yet a narrower term, is one type of acquaintance rape and describes a rape while on a social outing or in a committed "dating" relationship.

These legal definitions are important, but to work effectively with survivors of acquaintance rape, religious professionals need also to understand acquaintance rape as a psychospiritual matter. Spiritually and theologically, acquaintance rape involves bodily, relational, sexual, and incarnational violence.[10] First, acquaintance rape is the violation of *a woman's bodily integrity by force or threat of physical violence*. This invasion of her physical integrity and denial of her self-agency violates how she operates as a being in the world. Second, acquaintance rape is a violation of *a relationship*. Because the assailant knows the woman before the rape, any hope for mutuality or a just relationship is devastated. Not only is their relationship destroyed, but the survivor's other relationships are negatively affected. Third, acquaintance rape violates what Toinette Eugene calls a woman's *psycho-spiritual-sexual integrity* by using sexualized actions to control and express violence. Sexual actions become the means, and control and humiliation the end. This invasion affects the source of procreation, confusing what is life-giving and profound with what is death-threatening and soul-violating. Finally, acquaintance rape is a violation of the *Spirit of God incarnate* in each of us. The bruising and violation done to a woman's body are a bruising and violation of what is seen as representative of the Incarnate Spirit of God. With this psycho-spiritual definition, we begin to grasp the breadth and depth of a violence that assaults a person physically, communally, creatively, and spiritually.

Statistics reveal a reality in which many women have every reason to feel unsafe in their own communities. (That they ever felt safe remains in question.) Acquaintance rape has changed the image of the carefree life of the young adult woman. Young adulthood is a time for working on issues of identity and intimacy. Because of acquaintance rape, many women are forced to add to this developmental task the identities of victim and survivor.[11] Gone is the myth that young adulthood is the stress-free time of no responsibilities and a moratorium or "evolutionary truce" on adult issues.[12]

We know that, on a regular basis, women are the targets of sexualized violence. We also know that few report the violence. What this means is that acquaintance rape is closer to us than we are ready to acknowledge. For a small minority, acquaintance rape is just a name in a newspaper; for most, it is the experience of a coworker, classmate, friend, or family member. Perhaps it has happened to you. Acquaintance rape is shocking in its "normality." Yet there is nothing normal about it.

The types of rape vary, depending on the previous connection between the victim and the perpetrator, the amount of violence used, the number of assailants involved, and the number of simultaneous crimes committed. Aggravated rape is the easiest to identify and prosecute. This type can include premeditation, obvious violence, weapons, struggling or fighting back by the woman, and no familiarity between the man and woman. It is easy to identify the crime, the victim, and who is to be held accountable. Few question that this is rape. This type of rape, however, is a relatively rare event. The majority of rapes fall into the category of "simple rape," that is, with little public evidence of violence, a single attacker, and no other crime committed at the time.[13] While acquaintance rapes can fall under either category, the majority are classified as "simple." Aggravated rape is horrendous for its torture and obvious violence. Simple rape can produce many of the same physical and psychospiritual horrors and yet can be harder for the victim/survivor and others to accept as traumatizing. Some suggest that survivors of acquaintance rape may be more psychologically harmed than survivors of stranger rape because survivors of acquaintance rape more often blame themselves, do not interpret the assault as rape, continue to have contact with the perpetrator, and do not seek legal, medical, or psychological help.[14] Neither do they accept pastoral help. Survivors of acquaintance rape, whether aggravated or simple, also sustain physical trauma to their bodies that typically requires medical attention. Injuries sustained during the attack may include bruises and scratches on arms, legs, torso, and head; vaginal and anal cuts, tears, and bruising; mouth and throat sores from forced oral sex; sore hip joints; and more. In many ways a survivor of rape can look like someone who has been in an accident. But the aftermath is not the same.

The physical injury from a rape can be serious. It is a clear sign that what occurred had nothing to do with consensual sex. Survivors initially focus on the physical bruises and cuts. Acquaintance rape, however, can leave psychospiritual scars well beyond the visible damage. After the cuts and bruises have healed, the survivor is left to face the daunting task of surviving the psychospiritual effects of the violence. Fear, shame, depression, self-blame, and lack of trust are all too common. When the perpetrator is an acquaintance (date, classmate, employer, coworker), feelings of confusion and betrayal can be even more overwhelming than if the rapist had been a stranger.

Acquaintance rape is a crime that can cause pronounced psychospiritual trauma, by which I mean an all-encompassing response to an event resulting in a fundamental separation from self, God, and others. Such a psychospiritual crisis occurs when a person's embodied understanding of God and embodied sense of identity are together so traumatized that it destroys one's basic assumptions about the safety of the world, the positive value of one's being, and the meaningful order of God's creation. This results in a deep spiritual trauma that psychological tools alone cannot sufficiently explain. Understanding such trauma requires an additional theological exploration. Questions of consent, lack of safety, and feelings of unworthiness and betrayal are just some of the struggles a survivor faces as she attempts to reconstruct a holding environment that helps her "make sense." A survivor able to recover from acquaintance rape is one that attends to the psychological and theological issues specific to her trauma. She can find help in this reconstructive work from informed religious professionals. A survivor can be helped by religious professionals as together they struggle with understanding how she makes sense of the trauma and who she is in light of it. As we shall see in more detail, acquaintance rape is a direct attack on the survivor's ability to make meaning and have faith. Religious professionals can be important to this meaning-making work. The lasting effects of the rape and the psychospiritual centrality of the rape depend largely on the response of those around the survivor and her process of recovery. When a survivor's ability to make meaning involves the psychospiritual and theological issues of virginity, betrayal, theodicy, consent, and shame, informed religious professionals become crucial to the survivor's healing processes.

Voices and Metaphors from the Tradition

To be a trusted advocate and companion to a survivor of acquaintance rape, pastoral caregivers are required to stand in the midst of suffering and evil. This is never an easy task, and yet as people of faith we are called to be courageous and just in our caring, not comfortable and wise in our efficiency. The Christian tradition provides examples of both traumatized victims and just caregivers. As we start our work with survivors of acquaintance rape, it is helpful to look at a few of these stories, both for what they have to offer to the discussion of healing and for how their misinterpretations can add to the difficulty in naming the violence.

Texts of Terror (2 Samuel 13:1-39; Genesis 34:1-2)

The Hebrew Scriptures provide many examples that tell the truth about violence done to women. One need not be a biblical scholar to see examples of acquaintance rape. In 2 Samuel 13:1-39, we meet Tamar, the sister of Amnon, who is ordered by David to attend to the deceitful Amnon on his sick bed. Amnon lures Tamar into his bedroom, where, against her voiced protest, he rapes her. Stories like this are seldom heard from pulpits or in religious education contexts. When we do hear them, we hear an uncritical telling from the point of view of the men in the family. We rarely hear the women's voices. When we do, the story is changed from a story of violence to one of love and commitment. In her recent bestseller, *The Red Tent,* Anita Diamant presents a modern midrash of the story of Dinah (Gen. 34:1-2).[15] Diamant suggests that the relationship between Shechem and Dinah was one of love at first sight. The biblical text suggests otherwise. "Now Dinah the daughter of Leah, whom she had borne to Jacob, went out to visit the women of the region. When Shechem son of Hamor the Hivite, the prince of the region, saw her, he seized her and lay with her by force." (The RSV adds, "and humbled her.") Diamant's misinterpretation of a text of terror not only distorts the scriptures but ignores the violence done to women. To stop the violence and abuse of women and other oppressed groups, Pamela Cooper-White suggests that we do two things. First, we must hear the stories from the viewpoints of those violated. This is true whether the story is about the rape of a girl three thousand years ago or of a next-door neighbor in today's news. Recasting violence as love helps no one. Second, we are called to question all forms of authority and power that are misused to perpetuate, incite, or collude with abuse.[16]

The Good Samaritan (Luke 10:29-37)

Marie Fortune uses the parable of the Good Samaritan as a model for responding in a just way to sexualized violence.[17] In the parable of the Good Samaritan, we are clear that a crime has occurred, and we are clear about the identity of the victim. A man is beaten, robbed, and left at the side of the road to die. Two possible helpers/healers pass by (adding to the violence). With the violence and victim so clearly understood, the parable goes on to suggest that the Samaritan saw the victim, understood the nature of the violence, and responded. We are sure about the identity of victim, the nature of the crime, and the most caring response taken to attend to his brokenness. Without this clarity, this parable would not have such a strong theo-ethical implication: When your neighbor is hurt and needs your help, give her or him aid. With sexualized violence, however, we do not have this clarity. Like the compassionate Samaritan, we are called to go out of our way to help the one victimized. We can only help, however, if we know who the victim is, the extent of the violation, and how we can help. Using these lessons from the parable of the Good Samaritan, Fortune names the importance of defining forms of sexualized violence, identifying the victims, and proclaiming compassionate responses for religious professionals and church communities.

Wounded Healer

Pastoral caregivers can also find helpful models in the resources of the Christian tradition. Cooper-White turns to Henri Nouwen's metaphor of the wounded healer to discuss the caregiver's role in working with survivors of sexualized trauma.[18] This metaphor points to both the healing strengths and the perils in working with such a traumatized population. Caregivers who know trauma and brokenness can be most compassionately empathic with a victim. Because all forms of sexualized violence are "nonsensical" and often beyond words, the careprovider who knows about trauma can better accompany the victim on the path to healing.

The advantage of looking at the pastor as a wounded healer allows us to see the reality of how difficult a task it can be to work with survivors of sexual trauma. The experience of horror is contagious. Secondary or vicarious traumatization can happen to any pastoral careprovider who works with survivors.[19] Religious care professionals, as with other helping professionals, should expect to feel helpless, overwhelmed, and incompetent as a regular part of the challenge of the work. This is a normal reaction, even for experts with long years of experience in the field. Along with vicarious trauma, religious and other professionals working with survivors of sexualized trauma commonly experience burnout. Because the work is so demanding, Cooper-White suggests that religious professionals working in this field need to attend to their own stories of trauma to "bind up their own wounds" before trying to attend to others.[20] The work is challenging enough. Having untended wounds makes the work much more difficult and renders the religious professional less equipped to be effective in the midst of the survivor's needs.

In pastoral care and theology, the metaphor of the wounded healer has become a useful resource for empowering and challenging caregivers. Womanist theologians and caregivers suggest, however, that such a metaphor has limitations. The wounded healer metaphor names the starting place of the pastor as the place of brokenness and even weakness. Womanist pastoral theologian Marsha Foster-Boyd suggests that the most effective pastoral care comes not from working from wounds but from having survived them.[21] As such, we work from our strengths of resistance and survival.

Using This Book

Enhancing the effectiveness of religious professionals with survivors of acquaintance rape is the goal of this book. In a growing sea of work on sexualized violence, this book focuses on the psychospiritually traumatic effects of acquaintance rape on adult women in the United States. While acquaintance rape can be perpetrated by both men and women, as well as one offender or several at once, I will focus on incidents that include one female victim raped by one known male perpetrator. I do not consider marital rape in the category of acquaintance rape because both the wider literature and the legal system place that conversation under the heading of domestic violence. In keeping with a feminist research design, I asked each research participant to determine if her experience met my definition of acquaintance rape.[22] The only definitional requirements I set were that the survivor at the time of the rape was an adult woman (of consenting age), she knew the male assailant before the rape, and she defined the event as unwanted sexual activity or violence. All the women in this study experienced unwanted, nonconsensual, forced vaginal penetration by a man's penis.

Pastoral care providers working with survivors of acquaintance rape can include college chaplains, hospital chaplains, military chaplains, congregational pastors, priests, and rabbis. They also include trained lay professionals. This book will concentrate on guidelines for any pastoral careprovider or religious professional working with survivors.

I hope readers will share my concrete goals for this book: to learn about acquaintance rape from survivors, to construct a pastoral theological framework from the psychospiritual themes that arise from their stories, and to provide pastoral guidelines for faithfully attending to survivors of acquaintance rape. To begin to understand the experiences and needs of acquaintance rape survivors, I start with some facts and theories on acquaintance rape (chapter 2). Chapter 3 presents the rape and healing stories of four survivors. The chapter is organized in such a way that pastoral theological themes and guidelines begin to emerge. Chapter 4 examines the psychospiritual issues gleaned from these interviews in a more intentional pastoral theological constructive manner, uncovering implications for the practice of pastoral care and counseling. Chapter 5 puts this discussion into operation by bringing together this newly constructed pastoral theology, the guidelines suggested by the survivors, and care and counseling suggestions from the pastoral theological literature. Its purpose is to present concrete pastoral care and counseling guidelines for working with survivors of acquaintance rape. It ends with a list of referral resources for working with survivors of acquaintance rape. The work ends with some pastoral implications when violence is no stranger.

2.

Facts and Theories about Acquaintance Rape

The goal of this work is to understand the psychospiritual effects of acquaintance rape on survivors so that religious professionals can learn to be more pastorally helpful. To understand a survivor's experience, we need to take into account the larger sociohistorical and relational context of acquaintance rape. What is acquaintance rape? What are the sociocultural issues that set the context for survivors' responses? And how do survivors respond? It is with these questions in mind that I present facts and theories about acquaintance rape.

This chapter includes two related parts. It opens with a discussion of facts and distortions about acquaintance rape. Both the psychosocial literature and the pastoral theological literature on acquaintance rape use the practice of naming common distortions as a way of addressing the statistical facts and misperceptions about acquaintance rape. We need to know both the facts and the myths about acquaintance rape because they influence how a survivor comes to terms with the violence and works toward healing. In the second half of the chapter, I present three theories of trauma. The first is a sociohistorical theory on the connection between racism and acquaintance rape. I then move to a discussion of two psychological trauma theories: rape trauma syndrome and post-traumatic stress disorder (PTSD). This chapter sets one of the theoretical contexts for understanding acquaintance rape. In chapter four, I will explore a pastoral theological construct of acquaintance rape.

Facts and Distortions

Knowledge of what many women experience during and after rape by an acquaintance is crucial in helping them heal. Behind these truths are commonly held distortions about survivors' behaviors and desires. These distortions have a powerfully harmful effect in the lives of survivors, for they hinder a woman's ability to deal with herself and her communities. Thus, knowing both the truths and the distortions is crucial in helping women survivors. Religious professionals can serve as companions on the journey as well as watchdogs over the power of the ever-present distortions. For survivors, knowledge of the facts and the distortions can help them understand and name what happened and see the connection between their struggle to heal and society's impact on their recovery. For religious professionals, such knowledge can help us understand a survivor's experience and the truths of rape. This, in turn, can help us avoid perpetuating harmful distortions.

Fact: *Rape is perpetrated by people we know and in places that are deemed safe.*

The majority of rapes are carried out by:
- a known acquaintance (50 to 85 percent),
- in a familiar residence (61 percent).[1]

This reality is crucial to note, for most people think that a *real* rape involves a stranger who jumps out of the bushes or appears from a dark alley. One study found that as many as 90 percent of the women survivors they interviewed met their violators through social situations or through work. Over two-thirds (70 percent) of the women knew the assailant fairly well.[2] On college campuses, over half (57 percent) of rapes by an acquaintance are on first dates. Such statistics make the reality of acquaintance rape that much more unsettling, for, prior to the assault, the relationships typically bear no defining or distinctive characteristics to act as a warning signal. Apart from cases involving a boyfriend or ex-boyfriend, no sexual intimacy is implicit in any of the relationships listed. These statistics suggest that it would be safest to lock yourself out of the house and office during the day and avoid people you know and trust!

Fact: *Men and boys are raped by acquaintances.*

It is falsely held that only women and girls can be raped by an acquaintance. Because of the way the FBI conforms to the traditional definition of forcible rape, that is, as "carnal knowledge of a female forcibly or against her will," accurate accounting of sexualized violence against men and boys is difficult.[3] About one out of every five or six boys are sexually assaulted before the age of eighteen, and 9 percent of males are raped within their lifetime.[4] Ninety-two thousand males are forcibly raped each year in the United States.[5] Boys account for 25 percent to 35 percent of child abuse victims.[6]

Fact: *The charge of rape is not the cry of a scorned lover.*

Although the media and other social avenues of information would have us believe that the charge of rape is used by women to get back at unfaithful men, studies show that less than 2 percent of rape accusations are false. In fact, less than 2 percent of survivors of acquaintance rape report their assaults to legal authorities, compared to 21 percent of those raped by strangers.[7] Reasons given for not reporting include fear (brought on by real and perceived threats), guilt, shame, self-blame, lack of clarity about consent, the belief that it does not deserve reporting, and fear of police responses. A substantial number of victims (66 percent) said they would be more likely to report the rapes to the police if there were a law prohibiting the news media from disclosing their names and addresses.[8]

Fact: *Clothing, alcohol, and companionship are not signs that a woman wants to be raped.*

Fashion, social mores, and camaraderie are too often used as ways to explain a woman's culpability in her own violation.

Women's behaviors in social settings often have a moral quality attributed to them. Women's vulnerability is seen as a thing to deride when she is violated. Yet there is a difference between being responsible for rape and being in a vulnerable situation. A woman may be exhibiting a behavior that in a dangerous situation would make her more vulnerable to attack, and she may even act in ways that increase her vulnerability, but this is not a request to be violated. Everyone periodically acts in ways that increase their vulnerability to harm. When, in an attempt to cross the street, I walk into a busy flow of traffic, I make myself more vulnerable to being hit. I am not asking to be hit. I am asking to cross the street. On any given day, we each make decisions about how vulnerable we are willing to be in specific contexts. This does not indicate desire to be hurt.

A woman who drinks, accepts a ride with a man, or invites a man to her room is not asking to be raped. In the same way, stylish or even provocative clothing is not an invitation to assault. It is a statement of cultural and personal identity. A man does not wear an expensive watch because he wants it stolen; a woman does not wear attractive clothing because she wants to be raped.

Fact: *Warding off rape is not necessarily accomplished by struggling.*

It is a distortion to believe that women can always stop a rape if they really want to. There are those who believe that a woman asks to be raped if she does not fight back *enough*, get bruised or bloodied *enough*, and scream *enough*. When those who are in a position to help survivors believe this distortion, a survivor is left to defend her own victimhood.

> One survivor bravely confronted this myth during her questioning by a police officer after she was raped. The officer gave her his billy club and asked her to insert it in the Styrofoam cup he was holding. While holding the cup, he moved it back and forth quickly, trying to make the

point that if she had struggled she could not have been penetrated. The woman responded by hitting the officer on the arm with the club, causing him to drop the cup. She then inserted the club into the cup.[9]

The cultural bind in the notion of "You asked for it, so lie back and enjoy it" can be debilitating: Women who do not defend themselves must be "asking for it," and women who try to defend themselves are not feminine enough and need to be controlled. Either way, the woman's actions are used against her.

Built upon this double bind is the myth that her attempts at self-defense will result in her death. The confusion in this notion arises from studies that seem to "prove" both ends of the spectrum.

> A history of beatings and threats of another beating were held to be insufficient [as proof of resistance]. . . . Under the circumstances it would seem wise to advise a potential victim to resist her attacker since it is difficult to prove the existence of a contemporaneous verbal threat. However, such advice may place the victim in danger of serious bodily harm; hence, most rape prevention experts advise potential victims not to use physical force in resisting.[10]

In the end, self-defense and other forms of deterrence are the most promising. While no defense strategy is 100 percent successful, the use of no strategies results in a 100 percent chance of being raped.

Fact: *Nice and good Buddhist/Christian/Jewish/Muslim, etc., women get raped.*

Acquaintance rapists choose their victims without regard to whether they are good or bad, old or young, black or white, rich or poor, "Greek or Jew," religious or not. Acquaintance rapists prey on women they believe to be vulnerable. Morally upright women do get raped. So do immoral and amoral women. Morality has nothing to do with the victim's identity as a victim. When a survivor or her supportive community buys into this myth, both self-blaming and moral judging prevail.

Fact: *The majority of acquaintance rapists are not abnormal perverts or men with unsatisfied sex drives.*

Acquaintance rapists can have normal sex drives, may be married or have available and willing sexual partners, and exhibit normal behaviors. "Sick" or "insane" men are not the primary rapists. In fact, rapists can be understood to "overconform" to masculine stereotypes rather than deviate from them. Sex is the weapon for rape, not the reason. In the words of Audre Lorde, "rape is not aggressive sexuality, it is sexualized aggression."[11] The primary motivation for rape is not sex but power, anger, and dominance.

Paradoxically, the doer of such evil tends to insist upon a measure of self-respect. As William Ryan puts it, "in order to persuade a good and moral man to do evil it is not necessary first to persuade him to become evil. It is only necessary to teach him that he is doing good. No one . . . thinks of himself as a son of a bitch."[12]

Fact: *Rape is a conscious choice, not a physiological response.*

Once men are sexually aroused, they do not need to have sexual intercourse. To hold to the myth that men must have sex once aroused, is to buy into several assumptions: (1) There exists a "point of no return" once a man is physiologically aroused; (2) when aroused to the point of ejaculation, a man must have sexual intercourse; and (3) if a man cannot have sexual intercourse once he is aroused, he will somehow be hurt. Men may not be in control of their physiological responses to stimuli, but they do have a choice about how they relate to others when they are sexually stimulated.

Fact: *Alcohol consumption does not cause a man to rape a woman. Neither does it excuse it.*

Alcohol may give men "liquor courage" or serve as a disinhibitor, but it does not cause men to rape women. On college campuses, there is a high rate of alcohol and other drug use by both white perpetrators and white victims of rape (some reports estimate as high as 60 percent).[13] This, however, does not imply that alcohol induces men to commit a crime. It does suggest that these men and women are less in control when they are under the influence of alcohol and other substances. On predominantly white campuses, persons of color are less likely to use alcohol and other drugs; for women and men of color, the connection between sexual assault and use of substances is much lower.[14]

Fact: *Most women are raped by men of their own race.*

FBI statistics report that a great majority of rapes (93 percent) are intraracial. That is, most white women are raped by white men. The one exception to this intraracial finding is that Asian women are slightly more likely to be raped by white men than Asian men.[15] Media attention has greatly distorted black-on-white crimes. Unlike the stereotyped black male rapist, black men are not more likely to rape women, although they are more likely to be prosecuted for their rapes. Black women, on the other hand, are more likely than white women to be victims of rape.[16] Black women and other women of color are often more vulnerable to violence because of lack of community awareness, the necessity of working undesirable hours, high use of public transportation, inadequate police support, and not being believed.[17] In other words, it is not the color of their skin but their economic status that makes them more vulnerable. Women of color face a dilemma in reporting because it can mean turning to a racist law enforcement agency for support. Some women are unwilling to get involved with anything that may subject them to racist disbelief and blame.[18] Furthermore, racist attitudes about rape are so pervasive that women of all cultures are taught to fear black men.

This myth of the black rapist has an additional deep-seated effect on black men: society holds them to be inherent rapists. As a male student from Howard University said, "There's this idea in our society that black men will rape anything they see."[19] Working to prevent rape necessarily means working to end racism.

Fact: *Rape is always a crime but not always prosecutable.*

Acquaintance rape is particularly difficult to prosecute to conviction because it frequently comes down to the question of consent: They both agree sexual behavior occurred, but they disagree as to whether she consented to it. Rapists are rarely brought to justice, even when reported. For every 100 reported rapists:

- eight are arrested,
- seven are charged,
- three are convicted, and
- two receive prison terms.[20]

In general, acquaintance rapists receive minimum sentences unless they resorted to considerable violence in committing the rape. For this reason, very few women report rapes to officers of the court. It is therefore important for victims to know that conviction cannot be a reliable expectation or a realistic source for healing.

Fact: *Strong faith is not a deterrent to trauma.*

Suffering and recovery from rape are not a matter of having enough faith. When a woman is raped by someone she knows, she has been betrayed and is justifiably and understandably confused. Faith can be an important tool for her as she faces the pain of such betrayal. Faith is not a means to avoid trauma, but it can be an important element of the healing.

Fact: *The Bible can be confusing for survivors looking for clear guidance and comfort.*

Biblical stories can be a source of comfort for many Christian and Jewish women, but in its stories there is a lack of clarity regarding what a survivor can do to heal. Stories about the raped and murdered concubine (Judges 19) and the rapes of Tamar and Dinah can leave confusing and even negative images about surviving violence. Religious professionals should be sensitive to the reality that if women seek solace from the scriptures, they may need help interpreting these violent texts.

Fact: *Religious resources can be a tool for healing only when the survivor understands them as welcoming, helpful, and healing.*

Religious resources, such as biblical stories, prayers, rituals, and theological reflections, are not de facto life-giving resources for survivors. Even for survivors who have strong connections to communities of faith, such resources can elicit mixed responses. Religious professionals should be aware of their own motivation in using them.

Fact: *Religious professionals and communities of faith are not necessarily safe havens for survivors.*

Acquaintance rape is often misinterpreted as accidental or rough sex, and religious teachings can be quite ambivalent about matters of sexuality. In addition, a substantial number of acquaintance rapes involve the use of alcohol and other drugs, which religious professionals can understand as morally problematic. Because of these factors, communities of faith and their representatives may not be able to be empathically present to the survivors. When a member of a faith community is sick or has survived incontrovertible violence, it is likely that the faith community knows how to respond. When the violence is less clear, that is, when the survivor's behavior is called into question, signs of care and outreach are less available.

Understanding acquaintance rape means understanding survivors' experiences and some of the distorting myths surrounding the violence. These myths can have a devastating effect on survivors because even if they themselves do not buy into them (and many do), they must deal with communities that do. Learning the facts and the insidious distortions about acquaintance rape can help a survivor as she heals from the trauma. Religious professionals need to learn them so we can be better informed and, as such, become safer caregivers.

Next we examine how racism against African Americans has been closely linked to acquaintance rape.

Racism and Acquaintance Rape

Institutionalized racism creates intergenerational trauma. When generation after generation of African Americans have been oppressed by the violence of racism, their responses to the violence, and hence the violence itself, have become part of the communal soul. African American responses to traumatic experiences are dramatically influenced by this intergenerational trauma. There is little difference between the numbers of white women and black women raped by acquaintances, and yet evidence suggests that reporting rates, recovery issues, and communal responses are more problematic for black women. To understand this, we need to look at the role acquaintance rape has played in the history of African Americans. We begin with the defining institution of racism: slavery.

Slavery and Acquaintance Rape

Trauma and violence by a known assailant were the very basis of slavery. Rape by an acquaintance was one tool used to "colonize" African and enslaved women and, by extension, all Africans unwillingly brought to this continent.[21] The widespread sexual assault of enslaved African women and children was so normative that, for women, acquaintance rape and slavery went hand in hand. Indeed, slavery relied as much on routine sexual abuse as it relied on the whip and the lash.[22] (Virtually every known nineteenth-century female slave narrative contains a reference to rape by slaveowners or overseers.[23]) The rape of slave women was normative because slaves were understood as property, not persons. Devastation and death of a slave were thus handled as a property matter. When an enslaved woman was raped by a slaveowner, those with power viewed it as normal: How could someone mistreat his own property? If the rape was committed by someone other than the slaveowner, it was considered a property violation and, as such, trespassing. When named a crime, forced sexual intercourse was not understood and prohibited as sexualized violence but as miscegenation, the mixing of races.[24] The crime was not the loss of /the woman's or child's agency and self-determination but the loss of the purity of the white race.

The rape of enslaved African women bore financial benefits for slaveholders. In the eyes of the white owners, female slaves, appraised for their fertility, were not mothers, but instruments guaranteeing the growth of a slave labor force. They were breeders whose monetary value could be calculated in terms of their ability to multiply and increase the owner's net worth.[25] Children born into slavery, whether fathered by slaves or by the slaveholders themselves, became property of the slaveholders. With both African and European marriage practices being prohibited between slaves, and slaveowners' viewing slaves as property, owners did not recognize the state of "fatherhood." As a result, white society did not view children of enslaved women as family members but as additional property. It was in this way that institutionalized sexual abuse contributed to the devastation of traditional kinship structures. These structures were further eradicated by the regular selling of family members.

Emancipation, Lynching, and Acquaintance Rape

The patterns of institutionalized acquaintance rape and sexualized abuse of African American women were so powerful that they survived the abolition of slavery. The reliance on rape as an instrument of white supremacist terror continued to devastate African American families and communities in the post–Civil War period. The threat of rape, however, also took on a new role in the attack on African American communities. During Reconstruction, the rape charge against African American men became the most powerful means of justifying their lynching.

During slavery, lynching of African Americans did not occur extensively for the simple reason that slaveowners were reluctant to destroy their valuable property. Floggings were common, but lynching of slaves was not.[26] According to Angela Davis, lynching did occur before the Civil War, but it was aimed more often at white abolitionists, who had no "cash value." The number of lynchings increased as the antislavery campaign gained in power. With the emancipation of the slaves, blacks no longer possessed a market value for the former slaveholder. Freedom from slavery did not, however, mean freedom from violence. Instead, lynchings became a means of vigilante justice and a means to control blacks. It was at this same time that the myth of the black male rapist took on great energy.[27]

In the South, rape by "dehumanized black hordes" was the classic white male nightmare. White women's purity and matters of paternity became the justification for white male retaliation for what they believed to be the former male slaves' ultimate revenge: rape of the white woman.[28] By the end of the nineteenth century, Ida B. Wells-Barnett refused to accept the avenging of rape as an excuse for lynching. In her research, Wells-Barnett found that only one-third of all the cases of lynched people in her community involved accusations of rape.[29] Nevertheless, the charge of rape against African American men was leveled so consistently that the whole white nation took it to be true. Although the rape of African American women was pervasive, lynchings (and not rapes) became the most compelling symbol of African American oppression. The rape of African American women was overlooked. Even Susan Brownmiller's ground-breaking work calling into view the connection of rape and racism ignored the rape of African American women.[30]

African American Women Today and Acquaintance Rape
The legacy of rape of African American women in slavery and afterward and the myth of the black male rapist have had powerful ideological consequences for the African American community's participation in the current conversation about rape and rape prevention. Today the topic of rape within the African American community is seemingly closed to outsiders. The traditional response from the African American community to violence against women and children has been silence. This is not a silence that signifies acceptance of the violence, but shame, fear, and, according to Toinette Eugene, a "detrimental sense of racial loyalty."[31] Airing dirty laundry when the community is already under siege is dangerous. Turning to outside authorities has historically proved to be dangerous or, at best, ineffective. Turning to the African American community itself, women have confronted cultural myths (for example, the myth of the African American woman as oversexualized and promiscuous), internalized self-hatred, and, according to Eugene, a powerless or "benign" sense of justice.

Gail Wyatt asserts that because of the historical legacy of rape, African American women may be cautious about accepting changes in societal attitudes regarding their right to be protected from rape. African American women who are raped do not always see themselves as rape victims or their experiences as meeting criteria for "real rape." Thus they are not likely to name their experience as noteworthy to others. This has implications for disclosure as well as for initial and lasting psychological and physical effects.[32] When African American women do define their assaults as rape, they are still less likely to report them to authorities. African American women realistically anticipate lack of support from the community.[33]

First, African American women, more often than white women, are not believed when they report being raped. Because of the myth that most rapes are committed by an African American man against a white woman, African American women are not believed. Second, most of the African American women in Wyatt's studies report having had negative experiences reporting crimes. Consequently, they anticipate that they will be treated differently and blamed for the rape. This is especially true when the rapist is an acquaintance. Reality has shown that black victims of crime are not treated seriously, particularly if it is a "black-on-black" crime. (I find it telling that we have no category for "white-on-white" crime.) Indifference to black-on-black crime and the stereotype that African American women are promiscuous keep the rapes of African American women from being recognized and punished as crimes. Evidence has shown that prosecutors are hesitant to pursue rape cases involving African American women because society has an archaic notion that "good girls" do not get raped, and there is a prejudicial assumption that most African American women are not good girls.[34] A third reason that African American women do not report rapes is public reaction: African American women are more heavily scrutinized than white women. African American women are thus forced to deal with a historical connection between rape and racism that makes their avoidance of and healing from rape much more difficult.

Additional researchers draw the same conclusion: Reporting has costs deemed too high. Anita Jackson and Susan Sears suggest that for many African American women, interpersonal relationships are so highly valued in general that reporting an incident would be seen as damaging to the community.[35] Protecting the community is much more important when the community is a numerical minority, as on a predominantly white university campus. With the limited number of eligible African American men on campus, reporting one man to the authorities, even if he is guilty, is tantamount to turning against one's own community. When the community is already isolated and defined as "other," lifting up one member for sacrifice to a system that is de facto racist can be self-defeating. This bind becomes even more marked when we recognize that over 90 percent of rapes by an acquaintance are intraracial.[36]

From its historical foundation in slavery through the contemporary struggles of the African American community, rape has had a disturbing influence on the psychospiritual health of African American women and their communities. With this in mind, we are left asking, What are the psychological consequences for entire generations of women living under the constant threat of rape? When institutionalized rape and racism create such intergenerational trauma, trauma becomes a part of the baseline assessment for "normalcy." When acquaintance rape is both an intergenerational norm and normalized intergenerationally, at least two things happen: (1) Traditional definitions of trauma become inadequate, and (2) the psychospiritual trauma of acquaintance rape becomes a historical rite of inculturation. This has further implications for African American survivors of acquaintance rape. N. Duncan Sinclair asserts that when a horrific trauma occurs, those with compromised histories have an even harder time healing.

> No discussion of horrific traumata would be complete without an acknowledgment that institutional racism creates generational trauma that is indeed way beyond that of ordinary living. With this in mind, it is not too much to say that any horrific trauma inflicted on a person of minority status or a woman will have greatly increased effect due to the inherent trauma of racism or gender prejudice already present before the event and remaining even after the trauma.[37]

African American women have known acquaintance rape since their nonconsensual arrival to this continent. This history informs an African American woman's response to and recovery from acquaintance rape. Next we move to two psychological theories of trauma.

Rape Trauma Syndrome

The second wave of the women's movement in North America brought increased interest in work on sexualized violence. What did not exist, however, was an understanding of rape from the view of the victim. This was evident in the lack of information regarding the physical and psychological effects of rape on the victims, a therapeutic response to the victim, and protection from further psychological harm. Literature on rape explored why men raped, what role women played in these male actions, and the role of the courts. There was also a strong bias in the literature against women survivors' seeking medical or psychological help.[38]

In response to this lack of information, Ann Burgess, professor of nursing, and Lynda Holmstrom, professor of sociology (both of Boston College), conducted the first research dealing directly with the experience of the rape survivor. They observed that victims of rape suffer a significant degree of physical and emotional trauma during the rape, immediately following the rape, and over a considerable period after the rape. As a result, their goal was to learn about the immediate and long-term effects of rape as described by the victims and to develop a model of crisis counseling that met the needs of these victims.[39] Based on interviews and follow-up reports of ninety-two self-identified adult women rape survivors admitted to the emergency ward of the Boston City Hospital from July of 1972 through July of 1973, Burgess and Holmstrom documented the existence of a cluster of symptoms they termed the *rape trauma syndrome* (RTS). This was the first comprehensive theoretical model formulated to understand the experience of rape from the perspective of the victim. Through their research, they were able to delineate symptoms of and therapeutic responses to RTS and its two variations: compound reactions and silent reactions. *Compound reactions* to rape are a cluster of responses that combine rape trauma symptoms with either a past or a current history of physical, psychiatric, or social difficulties. Women experiencing compound reactions may also develop additional symptoms, such as depression, psychotic behaviors, and suicidal behaviors. Burgess and Holmstrom found that these reactions require long-term help and therefore fall outside a crisis model of intervention. *Silent reactions* occur when a victim has told no one and carries a tremendous psychological burden because she has not settled her feelings about the rape. In such cases, assessment of a victim's health involves helping her come to the point of naming her trauma as rape.

Rape trauma syndrome is "the acute phase and long-term reorganization process that occurs as a result of forcible rape or attempted rape. This syndrome of behavioral, somatic, and psychological reactions is an acute stress reaction to a life-threatening situation."[40] The syndrome is a cluster of reactions to a death-threatening moment or moments. Burgess and Holmstrom strongly assert that the symptoms named as RTS are not indicators of dysfunction or illness but normal coping responses to a devastating trauma. They are the body and soul's way of dealing with the unwelcome and shattering fear and trauma of the rape. RTS is described as a two-phase reaction, consisting of an acute phase and a reorganizational phase.[41]

Acute Phase: Disorganization
The acute phase (also referred to as "disruptive" and "immediate"), experienced over a period of days to weeks immediately following the rape, is characterized by general stress response

symptoms, in which physical symptoms are especially noticeable and the predominant emotional response is fear. In this acute phase, there are several categories of reactions: impact reactions, somatic reactions, emotional reactions, and invasive thoughts.[42]

Impact Reactions. In the hours immediately following the rape or attempted rape, a victim experiences a wide range of impact reactions, which fall into two equally evident categories. In an expressed style of reaction, strong feelings of fear, anger, anxiety, and distress are shown through behaviors such as crying, sobbing, smiling, restlessness, and tenseness. In a controlled style, strong feelings are masked or hidden behind a calm, composed, or subdued affect.[43] Whatever the specific reaction, the acute phase is marked by immediate crisis requests by the rape victims, which involve medical interventions, police interventions, and psychological interventions.[44]

Somatic Reactions. In the first several weeks following a rape or attempted rape, acute somatic reactions may occur.

1. Physical trauma includes general soreness and bruising from the physical attack of various parts of the body, including the throat, neck, breasts, thighs, legs, and arms. Irritation and trauma to the throat can occur for women forced to have oral sex.

2. Skeletal muscle tension includes tension headaches and fatigue. Disturbed sleep patterns, such as the inability to fall asleep or stay asleep, waking nightly at the same time of the original attack, crying out during sleep, and startle reactions, day and night, can occur. A disturbance in sleeping patterns can greatly add to the distress in the healing process, for it interrupts the body's ability to get on with the business of reparation. Jumpiness and hyperalertness over relatively minor incidents can be common.[45]

3. Gastrointestinal irritability, such as stomach pains, loss of appetite, loss of interest in food, or nausea related to thinking about the rape are common complaints. Nausea can also result from medications taken in relation to the rape.

4. Genitourinary disturbances of vaginal discharge, itching, burning during urination, and generalized pain are common. Some women develop chronic vaginal infections following the rape. Rectal bleeding and pain can occur for those women forced to have anal sex. These somatic responses bear witness to the real embodiment of the violence of acquaintance rape.

Emotional Reactions. Emotional responses vary from humiliation (often from forced anal penetration before forced oral penetration for purposes of humiliation), embarrassment, and being "overly cautious," to anger, desire for revenge, and inappropriate expressions of feelings (being overly emotional, flying off the handle, sobbing seemingly at nothing).[46] In Burgess and Holmstrom's 1974 study, fear of physical violence and death was the primary emotion described by survivors.[47] After fear, the most common emotions are numbness and disbelief. Self-blame is very common, particularly for those who had prior interactions with the rapist, and can have a long-lasting negative effect. Further, societal stigmatization is a common burden that only feeds the attitude of self-blaming. A fear of negative reactions and social ostracism is not unfounded. This is most common for adolescents who fear being stigmatized by their peers and being blamed by their parents.[48] Finally, because victims can experience such a wide range of feelings during the immediate phase, mood swings are common. Depression, however, prevalent in times of bereavement, is atypical of rape victims, especially in the acute phase.[49] If depression is experienced in this phase, it may be an indicator of a previously unresolved matter.

Invasive Thoughts. In the acute phase, invasive thoughts can be very disturbing. This can involve blocking thoughts of the assault or temporarily "forgetting" parts of the trauma. So much is at stake for the survivor as she comes to terms with the violence that the blocking can be an important defense mechanism for her continued cognitive and emotional functioning. This can have the effect of trying to undo what happened. This attempt to recover the former safety and security can fuel the attitude of self-blaming: "If I had only." Looking for responsibility can be self-effacing, but it is also a way to refuse to be seen as merely a powerless victim. The reality is she may have made some poor choices or even unwise decisions. Drinking to the point of blacking out, for example, is not healthy. In no way, however, does this mean that the victim is responsible for the rape. As noted previously, we all take risks and make poor choices on a daily basis. Yet we are not asking for terrorizing punishment in response.

Self-Judgment. Judging one's actions in hindsight, or "second-guessing" oneself, is another thought pattern that occurs in the acute phase. This critical judging and doubting by the survivor of her own intuitive responses to the attack ignores the fact that she probably did what she could in the face of a situation that presented few options.

With the strong emotions that do occur during this phase, a conflict between the survivor's emotions and her intellect can arise. This is especially true for a mature, aware woman who sees herself as well informed. She has a cognitive framework for coping, yet her emotions are mixed, intense, and beyond her control. This can be quite frustrating.

The time a victim remains in this acute phase varies from a few days to a few weeks. If the symptoms persist for a longer period of time, other factors may be hindering the woman's ability to integrate the knowledge of the rape into her self. In this case, the diagnosis shifts from RTS to a compound reaction, and a crisis intervention model is not used. Some women may never proceed beyond the acute phase.[50] More often than not, the acute symptoms overlap with the symptoms from the next, long-term reorganizational phase.

Long-Term Process: Reorganization

As the weeks pass and chronological distance builds between the rape and the present, a victim of rape begins to experience a need to reorganize how she lives in her world. The recovery task becomes that of restoring order to her lifestyle and reestablishing a sense of control in her world. The onset of this reorganizational or coping phase is affected by each victim's coping mechanisms. These include ego strength, social network support, and the way people see and treat her as a victim. The stronger the woman's ego strength, the wider and deeper her social support, and the more she is treated as a person with agency, the sooner this phase can begin. The length of time spent in this phase, from months to years, also depends largely on the victim's network of support and her inner resources, and on whether effective crisis intervention was available at the time of the rape.[51] Crisis requests by victims in this phase shift from physical and psychological interventions to emotional and supportive services.[52] It is during this period that a survivor is most likely to seek professional help. *Religious professionals who work with survivors are most likely to encounter them at this stage.*

Motor Activities. There is no standard pattern to this reorganizational phase. Changes in lifestyle or motor activities are often reflected in a change of residence, change of phone numbers, and variance in contact with family members.[53] Changing jobs or homes to ensure safety and to allow for some normality of behavior is common. This is especially true if the woman was attacked in her home or office. Her need for security may also include getting an unlisted phone number. The disadvantage of these changes is that by moving or changing phone numbers, she risks disrupting or losing supportive systems.

During this phase of confusing changes, many survivors will find that they have a limited level of functioning in their family, job, or school setting. They may need someone, for a limited time, to help mediate, relieving them of all but minimal responsibilities. Loss of "normalcy" is grieved. Establishing a routine can be important. This can help a survivor establish a sense of order and stability in what is otherwise a chaotic time. After a woman has been brutally reminded of the limits of her control, doing things that were once routine can help her reclaim and reestablish some sense of control. This can include going to work, going to classes, or exercising. Sometimes it means going through the motions until she can do it "for real." For a survivor who experiences her life as "turned on its head," reclaiming familiar routines can be instrumental in helping her reestablish her place in her world. On a college campus, this can mean the survivor continues to attend classes, even if she feels she is getting nothing out of them. The routine can help bring back the meaning.

Many survivors seek out extended family members for support, regardless of their previous degree of intimacy. They may visit a family member in another part of the country and may or may not share the information about the assault. They have a need to reconnect to a part of their lives that is somewhat stable, secure, and known.

For teenagers, truancy may be a response. They may see this as the only way of coping with responsibilities at school and with their fear of being stigmatized by their peers. A supportive, rather than punitive, response from parents, teachers, and pastors will help speed the reorganization process and the return to normal school and church participation.

Nightmares and Frightening Dreams. This includes both sleep-related nightmares or dreams and flashbacks or replays of the real trauma. Women report two types of dreams: one in which the victim encounters a dangerous person and wishes to do something but wakes before acting, and the other in which the victim achieves some mastery in the dream, either through fighting off the assailant or killing him.[54]

Traumatophobias. Phobic responses, or "traumatophobias," often occur in the reorganizational phase of recovery.[55] The most common phobic or hyperalert reactions are: fear of indoors/fear of outdoors (depending upon the location of the rape), fear of being alone, fear of crowds, fear of people standing behind them, and fear of sexual intimacy. The basis of these hyperalert reactions can be the very real fear of reprisal from the rapist. These reactions, which develop as a defensive response to the circumstances of the violence, are directly related to where the rape took place, who was there at the time, and how the assailant approached the victim. In the case of sexual fears, a disruption of normal sexual experience is common. For those women who had no sexual experience before the rape, the incident can be especially upsetting. When women have not had consensual sex before the rape, sexual intimacy can become equated with dominance, lack of control, pain, and helplessness. For those who were sexually active before the rape, the fear of sexual activity can increase when husbands or boyfriends approach them with desire for sexual intimacy.

Some survivors "regress" when they move into the reorganizational phase.[56] This involves a reexperiencing of a previous level of impairment following the assault. That is, four to six weeks after the rape, survivors revisit symptoms that they had experienced immediately following the rape.

Assessment and Response

The rape trauma syndrome is a cluster of responses to a disruptive lifestyle crisis, both in the time period immediately following a rape and in the months and years that follow. A caregiver for survivors of rape must take into account whether the survivor's response is RTS, the compounded reaction, or the silent reaction. For those who show symptoms that suggest RTS, a short-term crisis intervention model of counseling is most effective. Recovery from rape trauma refers to the survivor's return to a previous level of satisfactory functioning. To be effective, this crisis intervention model assumes the following:

1. The rape is understood as a "situational crisis" that disrupts the victim's ongoing life. Based on a crisis theory model of care, a treatment plan is based on the interaction between the external rape crisis and the victim's internal life-cycle crisis.[57]

2. The victim is regarded as a healthy woman who was able to function adequately before the rape.

3. The role of the caregiver is to help the survivor return to her previous state of functioning through an issue-oriented treatment. For this therapeutic response to be effective, the rape survivor should be able to maintain a certain level of equilibrium. No sign of ego disintegration, bizarre behavior, or self-destructive behavior should exist. This healing response is in no way considered psychotherapeutic. That is, the survivor's responses are not connected to a long-term, deeply-seated brokenness that requires attention to the reconstruction of the woman's core identity. This is a model of recovery, not a model of ego reconstruction. In those cases in which survivors have issues that require a treatment model other than an issue-oriented crisis intervention, referrals should be made.[58] In some cases, the pastoral care provider attending to the rape can assume a secondary function, especially if a previous therapeutic relationship has been established.[59]

4. Caregivers assume an active role in initiating therapeutic contact, as opposed to more traditional methods in which the patient is expected to initiate the therapeutic relationship. As we will see later, this short-term crisis model fits well with modes of care used by religious professionals.

Updates

Much has changed in the thirty years since Burgess and Holmstrom's work first began. In their 1974 work, Burgess and Holmstrom used the then-current FBI definition of rape: carnal knowledge of a woman by an assailant through the use of force and against her will. With the development of the field, researchers have opened up this definition to include men as victims, sexual contact not limited to penile penetration of the vagina, an understanding of force that could be present or merely implied, and the understanding that the inability to give consent (by lack of agency, ability, or knowledge) means no consent is given. Medical advances have introduced some changes as well. In 1974, medical interventions with rape survivors consisted of a gynecological exam, a five-day cycle of antipregnancy medications, and penicillin to protect against venereal diseases. Since then, the treatment for potential pregnancy has changed to one pill, and evidence collection has grown to include the use of high-tech equipment. In addition, the world has learned of AIDS. Now, the fear of death is not just related to the rapist's physical force and threat of force but also to the possible contraction of AIDS and other sexually transmitted diseases.

Limitations to Consider

The work of Burgess and Holmstrom suggests a stage theory to describe a woman's ability to cope with the effects of rape trauma. Such a model of healing has some problems. Stage theories, as a genre, generally move horizontally or diagonally upward. The movement is presumed to be linear, from past to present, distinguishable historically, or developmentally segmented. Stage theories are essentially progressive, moving ever toward or into the future. Because of their progressive nature, they are more concerned with change than constancy. Any movement backward is deemed regressive and developmentally problematic. By their progressive nature, stage theories imply that a valued destination is ahead (and only ahead), that change is desired, and that constancy represents a form of stagnation and failure.[60] Resting is the first step to backsliding.

An implicit assumption of the pervasive belief in stage models is the expectation that people will accept or recover from their crises. Contrary to this, studies have found that 26 percent of rape victims still do not feel they have recovered from their assault four to six years after the assault.[61] Yet in a stage model, women who do not move from their present phase of reaction to the rape are seen as stuck, or even repressed. Moving toward the reorganizational phase is seen as normative and healthy. Because recovery is expected, progression to the next stage can be encouraged too quickly.[62] This can be particularly problematic for religious professionals, who often can devote only a limited amount of time to a survivor.

By its very structure, a stage model of crisis intervention can shift from being descriptive to being prescriptive, pushing a survivor along a predetermined scale of responses. Such premature encouragement to move to the next stage can be received as unfavorable and can lead to frustration and disappointment. When we define "recovery" as adjustment or, as with RTS, reorganization, survivors can have a low "success rate." Success in healing should be measured by effective coping skills, through which the problem or resulting distress is reduced or alleviated.[63]

The rape trauma theory has some important further implications for religious professionals:

RTS Is Not an Illness or Disorder. Rape trauma syndrome is not an illness or a personality disorder. It is a normal response to an abnormally traumatic event. Rape survivors are normal people who can be helped by a response geared toward helping them regain their previous level of functioning. Demystifying rape and rape survivors allows mental health and religious professionals to work more effectively with them.

Importance of Social Support. Burgess and Holmstrom's work indicates that the most important factor leading to a survivor's relatively speedy recovery is her social support, that is, people with whom she can share her story. If victims have respectful social support from family, friends, or other intimates, they may not need any professional intervention. One of the most important things a religious professional can do for a survivor is help her identify people in her life who have been and can be supportive.

Historical Evidence of Pastoral Involvement. In the conversation about community programs for survivors, Burgess and

Holmstrom briefly mention a hospital chaplain program. In 1972, at the University of Chicago Hospital and Clinic, a program was established whereby, when a victim came to the emergency ward, a chaplain was immediately called. The chaplain provided support and medical information and acted as a buffer between the patient and the institution (much of what trained sexual assault advocates do today). The program was based on the notion that women need to tell their stories to a nonthreatening and supportive person as a "corrective emotional experience."[64] It was also believed that the chaplain's involvement provided a method of changing the institution from one that "patches" to one that treats people and their problems. For thirty years hospital chaplains have been providing support for rape survivors.

Methodological and Clinical Significance. My own pastoral work with survivors is significantly influenced by Burgess and Holmstrom's work both clinically (recognizing where a survivor is and therefore what type of care is needed) and methodologically (means of collecting data). Clinically, their work suggests that it does matter, pastorally, where a woman is in her recovery process when she comes to a religious professional. As noted, a survivor of acquaintance rape is more likely to seek help from religious and mental heath professionals when she is in the reorganizational stage of healing. Re-collecting her life and finding or making meaning of the rape now take on more importance than immediate safety issues.

The specifics of any researcher's method of data collection can make or break their work, and mine was directly influenced by the work of Burgess and Holmstrom. These researcher/clinicians did not presume to be disinterested number crunchers. In fact, they found that because they were interested investigators, survivors, hospital workers, and they themselves benefited. They gathered crucial information from survivors in exchange for crisis support and court support. With the hospital, they exchanged consulting services for permission to work on emergency wards, giving support to the staff and, in some cases, training the staff. Their research design highlights the mutual benefits of such exchanges, pointing out that research need not and, in sensitive cases, cannot be neutral.

Psychospiritual Reaction. Burgess and Holmstrom suggest that the predominating responses for a survivor in the acute phase are fear and self-blame. These are manifest in somatic and emotional ways. I suggest that there is an additional reaction—a psychospiritual reaction. Central to a psychospiritual reaction, in keeping with the other reactions, are fear and self-blame. Psychospiritually, fear and self-blame can be manifest as a sense of abandonment, doubt, loss of faith, confusion, loss of agency, and a feeling of disconnection from one's ability to make and give meaning to her world. The disorganization that occurs in response to the rape, psychospiritually, has both a "way of being" (ontological) aspect and "way of knowing" (epistemological) aspect.

Ontologically, a survivor experiences a trauma to her embodied soul[65] or bodyself.[66] Along with the physical, skeletal muscular, gastrointestinal, and genitourinary trauma, trauma occurs to the core of the embodied soul. When the soul has no viable options for integrating the trauma into its concept of God-center, it fractures. A woman's identity in relation to her community, herself, and her God is directly affected by the invasive trauma of rape.

Epistemologically, a survivor must face the confusion of not knowing what really happened, why it happened, where it is safe, and who can now be trustworthy and safe. What was once "common sense," or at least comfortably assumed, is now just one of many fuzzy options. A survivor can even doubt herself. How does she know she can trust her own judgment when her judgment could not assure her safety from rape? The traumas of being and knowing that accompany the other forms of trauma are real and deep.

Now we turn to a second trauma theory, post-traumatic stress disorder.

Post-Traumatic Stress Disorder

Post-traumatic stress disorder (PTSD), the diagnostic category initially created to describe acute reactive neuroses in soldiers, focuses on the adaptation of the individual following exposure to acute or prolonged psychic stress. War "fallout" was originally the emphasis. What quickly came to light, however, was that more women than men suffered from PTSD, and those women were survivors of rape.[67]

The earliest mention of any trauma-related reaction was in 1871 after the American Civil War. "Soldier's heart" (named because of the autonomic cardiac symptoms) was a disorder common to soldiers.[68] "Compensation neurosis," "nervous shock," and "hysteria" were also used in the literature. In World War I, it was hypothesized that "shell shock" was the result of a brain trauma caused by the explosion of shells. World War II veterans, survivors of the Nazi concentration camps, and survivors of the atomic bombings in Japan experienced similar symptoms, under the names of "combat neurosis" or "operational fatigue." With the influence of psychoanalysis in the twentieth century, it was hypothesized that "traumatic neurosis" involved a reactivation of an early, unresolved conflict by a traumatic event.[69] In 1941 the survivors of Boston's Coconut Grove nightclub fire showed increased nervousness, fatigue, and nightmares. This event marked the recording of trauma-related symptoms among a civilian population.

The psychiatric morbidity associated with Vietnam War veterans finally brought the concept of trauma-related symptoms into full view and articulation. Based on these early works, the world began to see that psychological trauma was a lasting and inevitable legacy of war.[70]

In 1952, the American Psychiatric Association included in its official manual of mental disorders, *Diagnostic and Statistical Manual of Mental Disorders* (DSM), a category for traumatic neurosis that described the disorder in a way that laid the groundwork for PTSD.[71] By 1968, the next edition, the DSM-II, approached the category of psychological trauma in a generic fashion, creating the categories of "Transient Situational Disturbances" and "Adjustment Reactions."[72] In 1980, the DSM-III included a new category called "Post-Traumatic Stress Disorder."[73] The similarity of symptoms across traumas was at last acknowledged. "Post-traumatic stress disorder" describes the symptoms that occur from

> exposure to an extreme traumatic stressor involving direct personal experience of an event that involves actual or threatened death or serious injury, or other threat to one's physical integrity; or witnessing an event that involves death, injury, or a threat to the physical integrity of another person; or learning about unexpected or violent death, serious harm, or threat of death or injury experienced by a family member or other close associate.[74]

Those suffering with post-traumatic stress disorder have experienced an emotional stress of a magnitude that would be traumatic for anyone, for example, rape, combat experiences, natural catastrophes, assault, and serious accidents. An adult's response involves intense fear, helplessness, or horror.[75] PTSD occurs when there is a normal emotional response (albeit severe emotional symptoms) to an abnormal or unexpected situation.[76] For a victim of rape or attempted rape, threat to one's psychospiritual integrity, threat of injury, and threat of death are common occurrences.

The characteristic symptoms resulting from exposure to a trauma such as acquaintance rape fall into three categories:

recurrent and intrusive memories, high avoidance symptoms, and high arousal symptoms.

Recurrent and Intrusive Memories

Lenore Walker suggests that, although only one of the types of intrusive memories is necessary to meet the criteria of PTSD, adult rape survivors typically report experiencing all four of the following:

Intrusive Memories. Survivors in the crisis phase, that is, chronologically close to the rape or experiencing acute symptoms related to the rape, are often overwhelmed by repeated invasive memories of the assault and the associated feelings of fear and anger. Ruminating about the rape, reliving it in her mind's eye while the survivor is at rest or engaged in unrelated activities, makes the rape ever present. Survivors further away from the rape may actually prolong the psychological effect of the rape because of the unwelcome yet constant thoughts of rape. These distressing memories may occur without any identifiable stimuli.

Recurrent Distressing Dreams. A survivor of acquaintance rape can experience literal dreams that recount the rape or indirect dreams of the rape involving symbols and metaphors. These may be quite confusing to the survivor. In the acute phase of recovery, survivors may not dream at all. Because survivors in this period often awaken before REM sleep, they are not able to achieve the state necessary for dreaming. As the survivor moves into the long-term resolution phase and is able to reestablish her typical sleeping patterns, her dreams begin to return.[77] Interpretation and normalization of the violent dreams may help the survivor's healing process.

Reexperiencing the Trauma as though the Rape Is Recurring. Common for rape survivors, this experience can be powerful enough to retraumatize a survivor. For those traumatized by multiple rapes, this recurrence can cause the survivor to dissociate.

The reality of PTSD is that the traumatic event is persistently reexperienced. This is one of the most difficult symptoms to understand. "To see that which is not there is a classic symptom of insanity."[78] The fear of losing one's mind occurs because survivors not only see it again but relive it again; their bodies remember repeatedly. To know the past event in recurring distressing dreams is within the realm of comprehension. But feeling the traumatic event is not. Those who care for and minister to survivors need to understand that the rape victim may repeatedly experience the assault in all aspects of all senses. To have a ten-year memory of the violence is one thing; to have vaginal pain ten years later is a different level of reality.

Dissociative flashbacks can occur when the survivor is awake or when she is intoxicated and can be triggered by either recognizable or unidentifiable stimuli. Consensual sexual activity following the rape can trigger these feelings of recurrence. Dealing with this may require changing those activities that precipitate the reexperience, such as previously enjoyed sexual activities. The survivor does not experience these recurrences as just a cognitive replay, as one might after watching a movie, but as a fully embodied experience. A woman's body remembers the fear and pain in a way that the mind cannot. When memory of rape takes on this visceral quality, there is no such thing as forgetting that the rape happened. That would require a complete body amnesia.

Anniversary Reactions and Other Conditioned Responses. Specific internal and external stimuli related to the rape can trigger both psychological distress and physiological reactions. Experiences such as seeing a man with a body structure similar to the rapist's or driving by the location of the rape can trigger both psychospiritual distress and somatic responses, such as rapid heartbeat and gastrointestinal discomfort. This can occur without a woman's being aware of the direct relationship to the rape. In some circumstances, such as bearing and rearing a child conceived during a rape, the survivor must find ways to separate her memories of the rape from her experience, in this case, of loving the child.[79]

High Avoidance Symptoms

After rape by an acquaintance, survivors meeting the criteria of PTSD will experience three or more of the following forms of persistent avoidance and numbing:

Efforts to Forget the Rape. Many rape victims will expend energy in trying to avoid thoughts, feelings, or conversations about the rape. This "forgetting" may involve a coping mechanism at the unconscious level, such as denial, minimization, or repression. Some survivors effectively "forget'" that the rape happened to them until something triggers the memory. For example, an older woman may "forget" that she was raped until she is called upon to support a daughter who has been assaulted.

Avoiding Situations That Remind the Survivor of the Trauma. Many rape survivors avoid activities, places, or people that remind them of the trauma. This avoidance of people can be problematic for women who live and operate in defined communities, such as colleges or military settings, or who previously deemed the community a safe haven in a problematic world. The very people who can support a survivor during her recovery can be the people who remind her of the rape. The associated avoidance behavior can have negative financial consequences for the survivor, for example, quitting a job because it is where she met the rapist.

Memory Loss. Survivors, especially those who have experienced multiple assaults, experience some type of memory loss.[80] In the acute phase after the rape, a survivor's hypervigilance can help her recall many details. Once she feels less controlled by the event, she can forget important parts of the rape. It is not uncommon for survivors to forget the linear order of the rape experience. This can be problematic when law enforcement officials take this confusion or "forgetfulness" as a sign of malingering or lying.

Apathy and Loss of Interest. Survivors can lose interest in previously enjoyed activities or people, particularly if they have any association (conscious or not) with the rape. This is particularly true for survivors who struggle with self-blame and shame. It can be easier for a survivor to internalize the rage, in the form of self-blame and shame, than it is to deal with the consequences of acknowledging that violence happened to her.

Estrangement from Others. Feeling like "damaged goods" can move a survivor to feel detached from others, often manifesting in a heightened sensitivity to minor slights or hostility toward friends who "just don't understand." Thus, paradoxically, she wants to be included but feels angry because she is not understood.

Restricted Range of Affect. Acquaintance rape victims may demonstrate a range of affect that is more restricted than before the rape: for example, the inability to have loving feelings. Because rape is momentarily a complete loss of control, some survivors reclaim their power through the grand "cover-up." Masking one's feelings behind a façade of composure takes an enormous amount of energy, energy that could better be used in cathartic honesty. Behind the patina of coping can be excessive stress. This stress can lead to more serious problems.

Sense of Doom. "Don't tell anyone or I'll be back!" "They'll never believe you, even if you tell!" These words, whether actually said or presumed, can terrify a survivor, giving her a sense of future dread or abandonment. This can result in the loss of expectations involving a career, getting married, or having children. Deep sadness, depression, helplessness, and hopelessness can accompany this sense of doom. The fears of death and of disbelief, triggered by the rape, can interrupt a woman's ability to dream and hope, two important elements of healing. The real possibility of sexually transmitted diseases, including AIDS, makes this response even more reasonable.

High Arousal Symptoms
High anxiety, especially panic attacks and anxiety disorders, is a common symptom for women experiencing PTSD. When these

responses take the form of free-floating anxiety and phobic reactions, they can be debilitating. Grocery shopping, taking the kids to the park, or even stepping outside can feel impossible. This is true for survivors of stranger and acquaintance rape. In the first few weeks after the rape, these symptoms can increase, creating an acutely painful and distressing "fear of anxiety." This fear of anxiety is more typical of rape survivors than other PTSD sufferers. Those who suffer from PTSD will experience at least two of the following symptoms of increased arousal:

Difficulty in Falling or Staying Asleep. Both commonly occurring for survivors, these responses are particularly problematic if the woman was raped in her own bed, or if she had been asleep right before the rape. Even the smallest amounts of sleep loss over time can be debilitating and can interfere with a woman's ability to cope with other symptoms.

Irritability or Outbursts of Anger. Many survivors, once they are able to become angry, do not understand their irritability or angry outbursts. It is particularly confusing for survivors and supportive friends and family when the anger is directed toward loved ones. Pastoral care can be an important way to address a woman's outbursts, focusing her anger toward the rape and rapist and away from friends and important relationships. It is equally important for family members and friends to understand that the anger, although often misdirected, is a part of the healing process. One college student found that after the rape she became so angry with her parents that she did not want to go home during semester breaks. This was particularly confusing and painful for her because she had always been very close to her parents.

Difficulty Concentrating. A short attention span and difficulty in focusing on a project can be quite disturbing to a survivor who is trying to move on with her life. Cognitive confusion can interrupt a survivor's ability to complete tasks that call for intellectual abilities. This can be particularly frustrating for women who have relied on their intellect to get them through hard times, for example, college and graduate students.

Hypervigilance. During the acute phase, images reminiscent of the rapist can leave a survivor constantly "on guard." This hyperalert response can be tiring to the survivor and can compromise her ability to cope in other areas. During this phase, a survivor may not be able to tolerate the company of any man she does not already know. Even well-known men may lose their trustworthiness. Although this hyperalertness will usually relax, it is important for male family members, friends, and pastoral care providers to understand the situation and respect the process. A man's trustworthiness may have to be proved all over again. This in itself can be a source of pain and anger for supportive male friends and pastors. When this happens, it is crucial that the men talk to someone who can help them process their feelings. Men as well as women who have strong countertransference reactions to a survivor's response should never try to process these feelings with the survivor. Survivors have plenty to manage without this added burden.

Exaggerated Startle Response. This response may last a long time and usually occurs in combination with other responses of hypervigilance. It can interfere with previous levels of spontaneity and playfulness, a reminder that playfulness presupposes a sense of safety. Raped eight years earlier, one survivor felt "overly paranoid" when she was easily startled. It became important to help her to understand that this jumpiness was a normal reaction and that her hyperalertness was her body's way of relearning the limits of its environment.

Assessment and Response

To meet the DSM-IV (1994) criteria of PTSD, a survivor must experience symptoms for more than one month in such a way that they cause notably significant distress or impairment in social, occupational, or other important areas of functioning (such as intimate relationships and spirituality). The onset of the symptoms is less important than their duration and severity. PTSD that lasts less than three months is designated as "acute" and more than three months as "chronic." When the onset is six months or more beyond the trauma, it is specified as a "delayed onset." Rape is not necessarily prescriptive of PTSD. In general, women who have good networks of social support are less likely to experience symptoms that meet the definition of PTSD.[81]

The DSM-IV also added a new diagnostic category to deal with responses to intense stress.[82] Acute Stress Disorder (308.3) describes an acute reaction to extreme stress that occurs within four weeks of the traumatic event and lasts for no more than one month. The difference between PTSD and Acute Stress Disorder (ASD) is duration. For symptoms lasting less than four weeks, ASD is used; for symptoms lasting more than four weeks, PTSD is used. ASD may predict the later development of PTSD.

Prevalence

Not until the political work of feminists in the 1970s did scholars recognize that most PTSD sufferers are not men in war but women in civilian life. Most rape victims who are evaluated at crisis centers and emergency rooms (94 percent) meet the criteria for PTSD within the first few weeks of the assault, and almost half (46 percent) still do three months later.[83] Seventeen years after the rape, 17 percent of survivors surveyed still struggled with reactions that meet the criteria of PTSD.[84] Rape and physical assault are more likely to lead to PTSD than other traumatic events affecting civilians, including robbery, the tragic death of close friends or family, and natural disaster.[85] PTSD is most likely to develop when traumatic events occur in an environment previously deemed safe.[86] Understandably, survivors of acquaintance rape are logically susceptible. While PTSD is not the only disorder that develops following exposure to extreme stress and trauma (other disorders include substance abuse, anxiety disorder, Acute Stress Disorder, and depression), PTSD is common for survivors of rape. In fact, rape victims may constitute the largest single group of PTSD sufferers.[87] It is not uncommon for private psychiatric hospitals to set up PTSD units that treat large numbers of rape victims, many of them victims of multiple assaults. This seems not unlike U.S. Veterans Administration hospitals that work with PTSD veterans.

Limitations to Consider

While PTSD is one way to begin to understand a woman's response to acquaintance rape, it in itself does not adequately explain a woman's suffering.

PTSD Is Unidimensional. PTSD is one way of understanding the psychosocial consequences of a survivor's traumatic experience. It can never stand on its own. In his work on post-traumatic stress, N. Duncan Sinclair asserts that the "unemotional tone of the technical manual" (DSM-IV) summarizes only the psychological effects of any severe trauma. Clergy, families, and pastoral counselors know that the effects of PTSD are much more pervasive, reaching every facet of human living.[88] Acquaintance rape is more than just a psychological trauma. Religious professionals should be aware of a variety of different theories (psychospiritual, statistical, historical, psychological) to understanding the survivor's experience of acquaintance rape.

Unidentified Symptoms. Many of the factors most commonly associated with acquaintance rape survivors are not indicated in the PTSD criteria. Not all symptoms experienced by survivors need to be considered as criteria for PTSD; but when the symptoms seem to occur repeatedly among acquaintance rape trauma sufferers, they should be taken into consideration. These symptoms include:

• Sensory distortion. Time appears to slow down during a critical incident, so that a survivor can feel as though things are going in slow motion. This distortion can occur in any of the five senses, although the most common are visual and auditory.

- Fear of insanity. After rape, a survivor can feel as though she is "losing it," and that she will never move beyond the horrendous shock. If this feeling endures long enough, a survivor can experience suicidal ideations.
- Sorrow, guilt, and survival guilt. A woman able to ward off a rape can feel sorrow and guilt when she hears of others unable to stop the rape. This can go hand in hand with self-blame.
- Exacerbation of existing life problems. Too often misdiagnosed as having a hysterical personality disorder, a survivor can experience an increase in volume of previous life problems. In part, this is because the survivor's normal coping mechanisms are compromised. If a woman was dealing with other major life stressors, such as divorce or ailing parents, rape may intensify the situation and force her to deal prematurely with issues related to the initial stressor.
- Sexual dysfunction. Because healthcare professionals regularly fail to ask survivors about sexual functioning, loss of sex drive or vitality is under-reported. This sexual dysfunction can traumatize a person, not as a side effect but as a part of the disorder.
- Suicidal thoughts and suicide attempts, self-medicating and evasive use and abuse of alcohol and other drugs, eating disorders, vulnerability to subsequent violence, and depression are also commonly experienced by acquaintance rape survivors in the reorganization phase.[89]

None of these symptoms is listed among the PTSD criteria, and yet they are common for survivors of acquaintance rape. As with all cases related to PTSD and RTS, it is important to know the range of symptoms common to survivors because, when survivors experience these symptoms and are not helped to see the "normalcy" of the response, they can feel additional shame and confusion. To treat some of these responses independently of their precipitant is to mislabel the problem.

PTSD as a Cultural and Intergenerational Way of Life. Sinclair alludes to the reality that, for communities of people who have been traumatized as a way of life, their responses to trauma take on a cultural and cross-generational magnitude.[90] This can look very different from the criteria supplied by the DSM-IV. The hesitancy to report, "over protection" of the community, prolonged mistrust of those in helping positions, and an unwillingness to name their trauma as noteworthy all need to be seen not as signs of regression or resistance but as normal responses to generational trauma.

Cognitive Effects. PTSD fails to acknowledge the cognitive effects of acquaintance rape. Persons not touched by violence can maintain beliefs about personal invulnerability, safety, trust, and intimacy. This is not so with victims of intimate violence. Many clinicians believe that victimization-induced changes in cognitive schema are rape's most disabling legacy.[91]

Value of Coping Mechanisms. PTSD does not take into account the positive value of coping mechanisms such as denial, especially at an early age. Denial can be a crucial method of getting past the acute phase of the rape trauma. This is true, as well, for dissociative experiences. Too often these are seen as completely counterindicated to healing.

PTSD as "Malingering." In the DSM-IV, one of the differential diagnoses for PTSD is malingering, "the intentional production of false or grossly exaggerated physical or psychological symptoms, motivated by external incentives."[92] The DSM-IV states, "malingering must be ruled out in those situations in which financial remuneration, benefit eligibility, or forensic determinations play a role."[93] I find this warning disturbing. PTSD and Acute Stress Disorder, two of fourteen anxiety disorders listed in the DSM-IV, are the only disorders with this warning about malingering. That the two diagnoses most often related to rape are qualified with this warning suggests that survivors of rape are making up symptoms and falsely accusing others of rape.

PTSD and Judaism. Jeffrey Jay suggests that traditional psychotherapeutic responses to trauma differ from those of the

Jewish community.[94] From this difference arises an important critique of such therapeutic models as PTSD. Jay suggests that, in psychotherapeutic theories, moving past the reality of a traumatic memory to "resolution," or placing the event in the past, becomes a way to work with survivors. The purpose of memory is to place things in their "right" order in time: The rape was in the past and is done. This is typically done in isolation. Judaism, however, moves *toward* memory, raising the act of remembering to the status of a commandment. Memory of the rape by the survivor and the survivor's close and extended community becomes a way of refusing the privacy of the shame and the loneliness. The pain of the trauma is added to the history of the people and the historical story of God's people.

Healing and Diagnosis. Even when a survivor no longer meets the criteria for PTSD, the pain continues. More a reminder than a critique of PTSD, the cessation of the diagnosis of PTSD does not indicate that the rape survivor is healed. It merely means that she no longer meets the diagnostic criteria. A survivor can revisit the pain and the trauma of rape well after the related feelings are deemed "normal."

PTSD as Culturally Limited. Myung-Sook Lee, in her work with Korean women survivors of sexualized violence, observes that, although she can see symptoms of PTSD among these women, without the societal recognition of sexualized violence, these women do not and cannot identify with PTSD symptoms as of primary concern.[95] Lee suggests that for Korean women, virginity and dramatic changes in relational life (on a scale from isolation to abusive relationships) are of primary concern. Attending to the hyperarousal, the numbing, and the intrusive thoughts, suggests Lee, is not as significant as attending to these other culturally significant matters.

PTSD and Rape Trauma Syndrome (RTS). Rape trauma syndrome is now considered a subcategory of PTSD.[96] Other subcategories of PTSD include battered woman's syndrome, child sexual abuse accommodation syndrome, battered child syndrome, sexual exploitation and harassment syndrome, post-incest survivor syndrome, and therapist-patient sex syndrome.[97] Walker asserts that PTSD is not truly an adequate diagnosis to describe all the symptoms experienced by rape survivors because it does not recognize the variation of responses that can occur over time. It is therefore helpful to use the additional descriptive diagnostic categories reflected in RTS.[98]

Cultural, historical, and psychological dimensions influence survivors' traumatic response to acquaintance rape. To this end, we have examined facts and misperceptions about acquaintance rape, a sociohistorical theory about the connection between acquaintance rape and racism, and two psychological trauma theories. Together this information represents a significant portion of the theoretical knowledge religious professionals need to be pastorally effective. Absent from this discussion is the theological conversation. We next turn to this task. Because a pastoral theological framework of acquaintance rape does not exist, the remainder of this work will focus on creating such a model. The primary source for this constructive work is the survivor herself.

3.

The Survivors

It is not merely an academic exercise.
Even when you want it to be.
At the conference, talking to a professional in the field of
sexualized violence, I was discussing some theological
reflections on acquaintance rape. In the process of the dis-
cussion, she disclosed her own recent rape and trauma.
It is never only academic.
It is always personal.
I was sitting at my computer on a Saturday afternoon,
making progress on my methods section, when in the
midst of milling over the intricacies of my research design,
the phone call came. A woman had been raped and was at
the hospital. The police were there. They were waiting for
the trauma nurse. Could I come? Was there any choice?
I clear my desk,
Clear my schedule,
Clear my head,
To write.
But rape has its own schedule.
It is never only academic.

In the first two chapters of this book, we have explored some
foundational issues related to acquaintance rape. We now turn
to the constructive piece of this work. Two of the goals here are
to construct a *pastoral theology* of acquaintance rape and to
develop *pastoral guidelines* for working with survivors of
acquaintance rape. To do both, we now turn to those most
familiar with acquaintance rape: the survivors.

In this chapter, we meet four survivors of acquaintance rape.[1] Each survivor's story is presented independently and includes some background information, a recounting of the rape(s), and the survivor's response to it. At the end of each interview, I asked the survivor if there are additional things I should know about her experience. I include these comments. I end each section with the survivor's ideas for what religious professionals and pastoral counselor should know and do. While this chapter presents, in a descriptive manner, the stories of four survivors, in chapters that follow, I explore some interpretations of their accounts.

Hannah

"He Got God, Too"
Hannah, a twenty-six-year-old white Roman Catholic woman, is entering her senior year at a university in the Southwest. She is outgoing and healthy-looking. Her demeanor is upbeat. Unless really pushed, Hannah "makes the best of a situation." Born in a small Midwestern town, she and her two siblings were reared in a supportive extended family. Hannah describes her early life as nurtured by "religiously conservative parents" in a "loving and conservative environment." After graduating from high school, Hannah took time off to work and play. For the next several years, Hannah lived with her family and worked in the entertainment business. During this time, Hannah started taking night classes at a community college and attending Mass at a Catholic church. In her second year of school, she moved out of her family's house and into an apartment with her chemistry lab partner, Rose, and Rose's boyfriend, Steve. Together these three lived the young adult lives of studying, preparing for the future, and partying. When Rose was not around, Steve would boast to Hannah about his sexual exploits and complain about how Rose was not sexually fulfilling. Hannah found this inappropriate and would change the subject or leave the room when

he started this conversation. Hannah never spoke directly to Steve about her discomfort.

The Rape and Initial Response

One evening Hannah returned home after a long and frustrating day at school. Rose and Steve invited her to join them for a dinner out. At the end of the dinner, Rose had to go back to school to do some work and asked Hannah to drive Steve home. Steve had been drinking heavily and smoking pot. On the way home, Steve once again talked about his sexual relationship with Rose. When they arrived home, Steve kept up the topic. Trying to tune him out, Hannah turned on the television and attempted to ignore him. Steve began coming on to Hannah, suggesting that if they had sex, no one would need to know. Hannah stated that "it was never going to happen because she had a boyfriend who would drop her in a minute if she were unfaithful." Steve then went into Hannah's bathroom, masturbated, and came out to get her. For the next two hours, Steve raped Hannah in her bathroom. Later, during the trial, Hannah proved that this was not consensual sex because she had refused to take off her underwear and her pants. Hannah does not remember the sequence of events that followed the rape:

> I called my [out-of-state] boyfriend up. Although I didn't tell him everything, he told me when I got to school the next morning I should go see a counselor and so that's what I did. . . . At first I wanted to file a police report. . . . I mean he's probably done it to other women. He's gonna continue to do it. . . . I didn't want to file charges because it doesn't really matter to me. . . . But I called the police.

The police escorted Hannah to the emergency room, where a physical exam—including a rape kit—was performed. The next day Hannah went to see her college counselor. She did not want to press charges, but the police escorted her back to her apartment so that she could collect all of her belongings. Having to gather her things quickly, she forgot some CDs, photos, and other assorted possessions, the most meaningful of which was a crucifix.

> I had a crucifix that my mom had gotten me one year for Christmas. I had it hanging high on the wall and as I was scanning the room I totally forgot it 'cause it was out of my vision. It was up at an angle hanging from the ceiling. . . . So, he got God, too.

In the weeks that followed, Hannah suffered physically, emotionally, socially, and spiritually. For several weeks, she had physical reminders; for two weeks, she could not stand up straight because of the bruising and was suicidal. At the time of this interview (eighteen months after the rape), Hannah still had a small scar on her face from the rape. She stopped going to church. She had to move back in with her family, from whom she felt little support. School was an ambiguous topic. It was hard seeing Rose, with whom she had had a good relationship, because Rose knew what had happened and was still dating and living with Steve. Before the rape, Hannah had been a top student. Going to classes now, she was distracted, weepy, and unable to concentrate. She was just going through the motions.

Several months after the rape, a time filled with suicidal thoughts, missed classes, and counseling sessions, Hannah decided to press charges. To do so, she felt she needed to move a safe distance away; Hannah believed Steve to be dangerous. After meeting with someone from the state attorney's office, she moved to another state, where she enrolled as a junior in a university. From the time she filed charges to the time Steve was arrested, Hannah lived in terror that he would come find her and hurt her. Hannah spent her first semester in her new home suffering from a variety of trauma-related symptoms and having no friends from whom she could find support. She could not remember her own phone number, she could not withdraw money from her bank account because she could not remember her PIN number, and she could not call her mother because she could not remember her number. "I didn't write Mom's number down because you should know your mother's number!"[2] She was experiencing flashbacks and having suicidal ideations. She was frustrated, alone, and scared. When asked about her healing, Hannah stated that she did not "cope," but, instead, just "dealt" with the rape. Coping, she said, required too much of a feeling of being in control. For Hannah the language of control and coping did not describe her healing either spiritually or experientially.

By December break, nothing had developed, and all her school friends were going to their respective homes for the holidays. Hannah did not feel that she could go back to visit family because she did not feel safe around Steve. She spent Christmas away from home, alone and sad. Almost eight months after pressing charges (and a year since being raped), Hannah received a letter from her attorney indicating that the case was going to trial. Steve's attorneys and friends kicked into action, trying to find Hannah's unlisted phone number and her location; they wanted to "convince her" not to testify at the trial. They started calling Hannah's mother, alternately harassing her and lying about who they were and what they wanted. Because Steve's attorneys were convinced that Hannah would not come back to testify, they offered a plea bargain: Steve would get counseling, pay for Hannah's counseling, and do some community service. Hannah's friends tried to convince her that was the best she could expect. This so enraged Hannah that any hesitancy she had in returning to testify disappeared.

> Fuck it; that's not good enough. No way. Community service and therapy? That's what I've had for a year. No way. I'm the victim.

In the end, the case was tried in front of the judge without a jury. The jury selection had started, but Steve and his attorneys knew his case was weak and so pleaded guilty. Steve, having served eight months in jail, did not have to serve any additional jail time, but was required to pay restitution, pay for Hannah's counseling, and write a letter of apology to Hannah's mother. At the end of the hearing, the judge asked Hannah if she wanted to say anything to Steve. At first she said no. This was the first time she had seen him since the rape and she was scared. When the judge asked again, Hannah changed her mind and let him have it.

> You know he wasn't as big as I thought he was. You know . . . "How could I let someone like you have all this power over me? You're so pathetic. You're never going to be anything more than you are now. You're such a loser."

Steve responded by lunging at her and had to be restrained.

The hearing was an important part of the healing process for Hannah. She was able to stand in front of the man who had attacked her physically, spiritually, and emotionally; she was able to see him as a pitiable man. Hannah later said that she felt empowered by the words the attorneys said about her and by her own ability to keep her integrity while speaking out:

> I didn't realize how much Steve took from me until I got it back. I thought such bad thoughts about myself. I really did. It was at the trial, when my attorney and the judge called me brave that I felt okay about myself.

"Cleaning Up Her Karma"
Hannah's successful and empowering court experience so enlivened her that she decided to "give back." To "clean up her Karma," she decided to volunteer. At first she turned to a rape crisis center. After experiencing a flashback while listening to a rape survivor, she realized that she was not ready to hear other women's rape accounts. She then turned to a Catholic-sponsored agency working with homeless children and mothers.

This experience was one of the things that kept Hannah going during the flashbacks and long-term healing; she found it to be life-giving. Through her own experience, she felt that she could relate to others' pain and, in so doing, could be more caring.

"The Worst Has Happened and I'm Still Okay"

For me to understand both the rape experience and her healing, Hannah felt it was important that I know she had been the "golden girl." She was the child in the family who went to college; she loved her job; and her family idolized her. Hannah felt she had a blessed life. Into this blessed life came the terror of rape. Through it all, Hannah was able to look at the rape and say, "The worst has happened and I'm still okay." In the midst of the pain of healing after the rape, Hannah was able to find some meaning. In her own words, "Evil exists but does not prevail." This affirmation stemmed from Hannah's religious faith, which was grounded in a strong individual commitment to a God who is present and constant. This stands in stark contrast to her declaration that "He got God, too." Well after the rape, Hannah found comfort in the words different priests shared with her: You do not have to be perfect. According to Hannah, this requires "an ability not to think too much and to let go of control."

Negative Effects on Future Intimate Relationships

While Hannah felt that she remained strong in her faith, she continued to experience the damaging consequences of the rape. Before the rape, Hannah had had consensual sexual intercourse. She had enjoyed these relationships. Sexual intimacy changed after the rape.

> After the rape, sex changed a lot for me. I was sexually active before I was raped, but now when I date, I kind of judge the relationship by whether this is someone I could tell about the rape. It's not something I tell a lot of people about. If I have a sense the rape might be a

problem, I tell them right away to weed out those who can't take it.

Her rape story has, in fact, become a litmus test for relational suitability. At the time of the interview, no one had passed the test.

"It's No Big Deal" and "It's Not an Incident"

Throughout the interview, Hannah made comments that seemed to minimize her experience. When asked what she would do in the event that this interview brought up strong negative emotions, Hannah indicated,

> It's just an event that happened. You know, so I've had a lot of events in my life. This is just another event . . . it's fine.

As I listened to her talk, my initial assessment was that she was minimizing the enormity of the situation. This is not uncommon for rape survivors in both the acute and reorganizational phases. The more I listened to Hannah, the more I began to wonder if this so-called minimization was her way of trying both to face and find meaning in the violence. Traditionally speaking, minimization can be a denial mechanism: It wasn't that bad. Was she minimizing her situation or trying to make sense of it, a small dose at a time?

Although I wondered about the minimization of her healing process, Hannah was very clear about the rape itself. This was not to be minimized. When I asked Hannah what language she would like me to use in referring to her rape, she responded,

> Just don't call it an "incident." Anything else is fine. There was a school nurse who called the rape an "incident." An incident is when someone gets pulled over for speeding. This wasn't an incident.

Hannah's Suggestions for Religious Professionals

Hannah was very interested in talking about what religious professionals should and should not do for survivors. Although she could clearly state what she thought priests should do generally, these suggestions did not always match her own pastoral needs.

1. Hannah was clear about hugs and touching. When I asked her directly about how a priest might respond to a rape survivor, Hannah quoted a priest, "When you don't know what else to do, hug the person in need." When I asked if that meant a priest's hug would have been helpful to her, she responded with a strong no. She definitely did not want to be touched by most people, even a year after the rape.

2. Simple is the best; believe the survivor.

3. Do not minimize the rape.

4. Do not talk about God or God's love. When a person does not love herself, it is hard for her to believe that someone else loves her. Hannah felt that sometimes religious professionals throw in a "Jesus loves you" because of their own needs and anxieties.

5. Hannah blamed herself for the rape for a long time and needed to know she was not at fault.

6. Hannah was mixed about her feeling of loneliness through the trial process. She feels the trial was that much harder because she did not let people know what was going on: She flew across the country on her own, she sat through the trial with no family or friends present, and she lived in fear all by herself. As she reflects back on her "victory," she sees her lonely survival as a sign of her strength. She is sad about the loneliness and, at the same time, proud and empowered by the knowledge that not only did she survive the trial by herself, but she also won.

7. Hannah found comfort in words a priest shared with her, that she did not have to be perfect.

8. Hannah spoke very highly about the secular counselors she had seen. At a crucial point, a counselor was the only sup-

port person she had. Hannah did not make a connection between her counselor and a clergyperson.

Hannah was raped by a housemate in their home. The losses she experienced were profound. Her courage to press charges and her success in court strengthened her voice and moved her to give something back to the community. Hannah learned that she could not only survive the violence of acquaintance rape, but also learn about herself in the healing process.

Debra

"Finishing the Work of Dinah and Tamar"
Debra is a forty-six-year-old African American woman who lives and works in the Southwest. Debra was born in a Midwestern industrial town, loved by her mother, aunt, and uncle, and reared in the close-knit community of a black Missionary Baptist Church. Debra spent most of her social time around church-sponsored events. Her participation included singing in church choirs that drew from black congregations across the region. Debra said that she felt connected to and, at the same time, hemmed in by this outstretched church community.

Coming into adolescence in the late 1960s, a time when racial tensions in a river town north of the Mason-Dixon line were high, Debra's sense of safety grew out of her community and neighborhood connections.

> The way I grew up, we watched out for each other. Because I was the youngest of my peers, everyone watched out for me.

Her small, predominantly black community was such that few secrets were kept. She felt safe in her community. The schools she attended were mostly white, but she felt safe because of her connection to the black community.

The Rapes and Immediate Responses

Debra was raped twice, at ages seventeen and eighteen, by her first boyfriend. She trusted him. "He was very dark and had the prettiest smile." Because the town was small, everyone knew that he was also dating another girl. Debra and this young man were frequently together, although her mother did not want her to date him. As a result, they had to behave as though they were not dating.

The first time Debra's boyfriend raped her, they were going out on a secret date. She knew something was different about that night because he took her to a place where they had never been. In her own car, he raped her because he thought she was sexually active with other young men. That infuriated him. He did not believe she was a virgin. As she tried to convince him of this, he began to physically threaten her. This was so out of character for their relationship that it confused her. While he raped her, he kept asking, "Isn't it good?" and demanded a response. When the breaking of her hymen brought a flow of blood, he realized that she had been telling the truth.

Later that evening, Debra was with a girlfriend, crying in the car. Debra did not tell her friend that she had been forced to have sexual intercourse. Debra told no one about the rape until years later. Not telling family and friends was a personal defense. "I think that it is a safety mechanism because you don't want to deal with it." For Debra, this also meant not reacting to it. She was just trying to maintain her composure so that nobody would know.

For a week, she nervously waited for her period. Pregnancy was not something she wanted to face. When her period came, she was relieved: She was not pregnant, and she would not have to explain how she became pregnant.

Days after the rape, Debra acted as though nothing had happened; this included going over to the young man's house and "hanging out" with his siblings. She went to extremes so that nothing would change. "I couldn't afford to have anybody know." If people knew, everything would change. She did not feel this change would be safe until she moved away from her home and the area.

Throughout the devastating feelings after the rape, she did not tell her mother or aunt. Not telling was her attempt to control what was happening. Family and friends noticed that she changed and wondered what was going on, but she would not tell them. She felt that telling her family was tantamount to telling the community, and her community was so small that once the news was revealed, it would spread. She feared that if the community and her family knew, they, too, would fall apart.

> I had to keep this secret. I had to protect everybody. I didn't want anybody to worry and therefore I was all alone. I loved this man and I had a relationship with this man. I was close to members of his family. Everybody knew each other in [the community] and three nearby communities. All of the blacks, we hung together; we knew each other. If I told, everything would fall apart. If I couldn't hold it together, everything would fall apart. So I took on all of it. I wasn't about to let the world that I knew fall apart. So, whatever it took and whatever I had to do . . . I kept playing the same role even after the rape.

One year later, Debra was raped again by the same man. She had not told anyone about the first rape and was working hard to keep up the appearance that all was well.

> The second time we went to the park. I really don't know why he raped me the second time, other than the fact that I wouldn't have sex . . . or he was mad that he raped me the first time. I have no clue why the second time.

The second rape was even harder for her to deal with (and make sense of) because she felt more to blame. She was so invested in having no one suspect anything that she felt her "normal" behavior with him had invited the rape.

Long-Term Healing

After the rapes and for many years, Debra found that her own believability became her biggest concern. The rape had cast a shadow on her own self-perception, and now she had to make up for it. She became more reserved and more serious because "serious" was believable. Physically, she changed her posture to reflect a more rigid and serious attitude. She carried herself in such a way that no one would question her. She never smiled. Because "being wrong gives people reason to disbelieve," she worked hard at never being wrong. To Debra, perfection guaranteed control.

Control was a central theme for Debra. She needed to be in control. To be out of control was dangerous. When things weren't in control, bad things happened. In a time and place when white racism could be lethal, keeping control in the community was a matter of survival. For Debra, interpersonal control was directly related to this larger reality. In her account, she suggests that when there is little control, things fall apart, and that is dangerous, even deadly. On an interpersonal level this may seem extreme. But given the time frame and social realities, this hypervigilance would have been crucial for survival.

Debra did not talk about the rapes for well over twenty years. When she started talking to counselors, friends, and her pastor, it helped her come to terms with both the rapes and her response to them. With practice, Debra became more comfortable in telling people. Now she realizes that she has two reasons for telling. First, she tells of her rape experience to help young girls who are faced with a similar struggle. Second, and only recently, she realizes that she uses her story as a way to test the trustworthiness of the hearer. "You have to see where people are with the hearing of it. If they can handle the story of the rapes then they can handle me."

Despite the fact that Debra has found a constructive use for her story, the rapes have still had painful consequences for her life. Debra was in love with the young man who raped her. Every potentially intimate relationship since the rapes has been negatively affected. She is quite conflicted about the whole thing.

> I had feelings for him for a long time, even after what he did to me. I tried calling him but he would not talk to me, and that made me feel small and angry.

The last time she saw the man was at a party for his father. There, she said she tried to "seduce" him because she was so mad at him. It was only much later that she began to understand her behavior. She was mad at him, and the retribution of using him as he had used her seemed justifiable.

During the first rape, her boyfriend continually asked her, "Isn't it good?" In her sexual encounters since that time, she finds herself asking her partners if she is good. Debra believes these are related.

> I think I had it in my mind that I had to be good. I had to perform. It was always a performance. It was never an enjoyment. It was two edges of a blade: I would get hurt or they wouldn't love me if I didn't perform well. So it was a performance.

After the rapes she did not want to have sex. The first consensual sex she had, she felt nothing. She remembers it as a blur. Debra has had no lasting relationships, and she attributes this fact to the rapes.

Since the rapes, Debra has had a strong negative reaction to men with dark skin; they physically remind her of her rapist. This issue becomes more complex with the realization that skin color is already an issue within the African American community.

We have prejudice within the black community with color. I only like the lighter color Afro-race because the guy who raped me was dark. And to me, the darker you are the more afraid of you I am. I wasn't like that before the rape. I didn't make the connection until much later. My mom and my aunt are all dark. My uncle and my biological father weren't. My mom said, "You know, the blacker the berry, the sweeter the juice." But for me, I thought, "You don't know the black berry that I had." There was nothing sweet about him.

Anger, Revenge, and Forgiveness

For years after the rapes, Debra was angry and felt the need for revenge. Initially, she tried to seduce the man who raped her— to use him as she had been used. When this did not work, she felt even worse about herself. In her attempt to gain control of the situation, Debra internalized the anger; she "stuffed it." Debra used three powerful images to describe the presence and force of her anger:

Anger was always like my peripheral vision . . . like a stalker . . . like clouds always there. Getting rid of that anger means the peripheral vision is clear.

To begin the process of healing, Debra had to start getting rid of her anger. It had to be an active process of getting rid of it, not just letting it go; she could not just "let go" of peripheral vision, a stalker, or clouds. For Debra, moving beyond the anger meant letting go of control. It meant "being able to disclose that part of me is not good." Debra felt that part of herself, even her soul, was tainted by the anger. This made her "sinful." In naming her anger, Debra felt very vulnerable. Debra is still actively working on moving beyond the anger.

Debra understood that, to be freed from the anger, she had to work on forgiveness. Unlike the other survivors in this work, Debra had lived almost thirty years with anger over her rapes.

For her, forgiveness was an important resource for her freedom. It was something she believed she ought to do. It was something that she did not do easily. She struggled with this process of forgiveness because it was never a part of her life growing up. She did not experience forgiveness as an everyday part of her life.

Years after the rape, her pastor introduced her to the idea of forgiveness. She was grateful for this. She had felt so consumed by her need for revenge that she felt imprisoned:

> Forgiveness is connected to being freed from the feeling that you are in prison. You thought you were creating a prison for everybody else, but then you look up and you are the only one in it.

Debra's anger and need for revenge were all-consuming. Coming to terms with that and the need for forgiveness were the hardest things for her.

At some point in her healing, Debra became aware that she was angry at God. She grew up with a fear of God. She believed that God knew when you were bad, and "God don't like ugly" (so her mother and aunt insisted). "God was never even a part of my rape. I guess God was sent to some sideline." Debra was angry with God for this. This anger contributed to her feelings of imprisonment, an experience she wants to help others avoid.

> I don't want anyone else to get caught in the trap that I did. You can be angry with God, but go ahead and tell him what you're angry with him about. At some point you have to deal with your stuff.

Virginity, Grieving, and Freedom

Alongside Debra's anger, grieving has been a necessary part of her recovery from the acquaintance rapes. One of the things she grieves is the loss of her virginity.

I never had the opportunity to choose who I gave my virginity away to. That opportunity was taken from me. . . . We deserve to grieve that which is taken from us. I'll never be a virgin again. I'll never be able to offer my husband the opportunity of being the first. I'll never be given that chance. It was taken away from me as someone else's [choice], regardless of whatever his reasons were. I had a choice and at sometime or other I would have made that choice on my own.

Grieving is much more than a signal of loss for Debra. It is a recognition that she has worth.

Claiming that we have something worth grieving is important. It is the starting point of grieving, regardless of the trauma. Feeling sorry and grieving is not a place to stay, but it is a place you are allowed to go. . . . Coming to the realization that I have worth is important. One of the best things we can do for each other is give worth. Grieving allows you to come to that point.

Debra takes it one step further in that she also believes grieving leads to freedom. She therefore suggests we need both to help people grieve and to teach them to do it. "Teaching grieving is necessary. You can't experience freedom unless you grieve." Debra found her pastor to be a helpful companion in her grief.

Once Debra had explored with her pastor the emotional and spiritual issues surrounding the rapes, she experienced a purging that left her feeling empty. This emptiness left her feeling depressed and uncomfortable. Healing, for Debra, included both purging the feelings she had suppressed for so long and replacing them with life-giving feelings.

Healing requires getting some type of help so they can move on, and putting some good stuff there that will help you and not hinder you. I think when I personally went through getting rid of all the stuff that had to do with the rape, I felt empty. I was depressed because I felt so empty. . . . I had to trust my choices about what to put back in. That first purge left me with such an empty feeling that I desperately wanted to hold onto something good or bad just to fill up the empty.

Healing as a Legacy from Dinah and Tamar

Debra found that something, that life-giving "stuff" in biblical stories. Dinah[3] and Tamar[4] have been very important to Debra because they too were survivors.

> Dinah never got as far, that is, healing. She just disappeared, much like David's daughter Tamar just disappeared; there's just no completion. So we're left still trying to resolve it. It's like a legacy handed down. Not such a good one, but it's one that we need to complete.

Debra sees her work of healing as a legacy; a chance to give back to Dinah and Tamar what they have given to her. They never had the chance to tell their own stories and demonstrate that they survived and thrived beyond their rapes. Debra wants to finish the work of Dinah and Tamar by surviving and telling her story.

"Letting Go of the Storm"

Metaphors are a powerful way of describing an intense experience, and for Debra, the image that viscerally reflected the rapes and her long recovery was a raging storm.

> It was a storm that night that destroyed my life. It's always been a storm. . . . I wore myself out trying to control that storm. In trying to put back all the pieces and order them around, I wore myself out. Healing is trying to find that space in the midst of it all where I can still be safe from the storm. The storm doesn't last forever.

The rape was the beginning of the storm that shattered her life. Immediately following the rape, explained Debra, the storm "roared like hell for a few weeks." When she tried to control her inner storming, things went wrong. Telling no one about the rape was her attempt to control the storm. It did not work.

> Trying to hold [the storm] in means it never gets to pass. I'm so busy trying to control it that it never gets to pass. The rape was the shattering of a storm and for over twenty years I tried to calm that storm. . . . You can't run. The more you run, the worse it is. You can't hold it back; it's hard enough that you're caught.

She marvels now that she thought she could keep the storm from running its course. She now sees her role as being in the storm with others and helping them know that there is a place beyond the storming. Debra is clear that, when she was in the midst of the storm, she could not have heard any words of comfort that implied "good could come out of this." She has been able to find meaning in her own struggle, but she is clear that she could not have been pushed there by someone else.

Debra's Suggestions for Religious Professionals

Debra has had many years to reflect on her rapes, her brokenness, and the role supportive people can play and have played in her healing process. Because Debra has had a strong connection to faith communities and pastors, she had a lot to offer when I asked her about the role religious professionals can play with survivors:

1. Pastors need to know their limits. To Debra, a pastor's ability to be helpful is determined by support from members of the congregation, information they learn from survivors, their willingness to recognize their limits, and connections they have with supportive community agencies. For Debra, a referral system is a must.

2. Pastors must be willing "to go to the tough places and hear the hard stories." To do this, they need to be open to God with a true willingness. "I know some of the stories of rape are unbearable, but if pastors call themselves theological students of the Bible, they have to be willing to go there." Debra was strong in asserting that a pastor's role is not just "taking care of the pretty women, but listening to the hard stories."

   Rape is not easy for the survivors, and it's not easy for the family. It's not easy for anyone—the people at the rape prevention center, counselors, or others involved in this area of work. And it will not be easy for pastors. That does not mean it is not their responsibility. Debra is aware that many religious professionals may not know how to help survivors. She suggests that, at some level, this response is a natural one. Nevertheless, "clergy should not turn their backs on it. If it were your daughter or your wife, you wouldn't." Pastoral work with survivors means sticking with it and knowing when to refer.

3. Pastors should not have an "attitude" about rape, that is, that it is somehow outside their responsibilities.

4. Pastors should not judge: They should listen and be "with" the survivor.

   > Even if I had been angry with God, listen. Hold on to the hope that the survivor can change, but let her be right where she is. Whatever space I am in at the moment, be there with me and don't be afraid to be there with me. Listening is the most important thing. You can't figure out what is wrong unless you listen. Listening with your heart, listening and caring. Finding a space to do that, and then be in it, is one of the greatest gifts pastors can give.

5. Once they have listened and heard, pastors should set up resources in the church and work in tandem with those community agencies set up to work with survivors. This can

include sponsoring rape prevention trainings. Debra was aware of one church community that, through the leadership of the pastor, provided financial support for survivors to see a counselor. The survivors were then asked to come back and be in conversation with the pastor about things they were doing with the counselor. Debra likes the idea of the pastor keeping involved in the survivor's healing process.

Debra is clear that pastors and rape crisis centers working together is the best way to support survivors. Even if they are well trained, pastors do not have all the resources to meet survivors' needs (time, knowledge, connections, etc.).

Debra was raped in the context of a close community. She told no one because she believed that the truth would endanger the community and her place in it. Thirty years after the rapes, Debra is able to speak about her difficult healing in creative ways. Her ability to reflect on her healing has given her the courage to help others in their suffering. Debra believes that religious professionals can play an important role in a survivor's recovery.

Melanie

"I've Never Attached 'the Word' to It"

Melanie is a twenty-two-year-old white Southern woman who is a senior at a Midwestern university. She is quite close to her only brother, also at the university, and her two professional parents. She describes her parents as stable, loving, and having the "perfect relationship." Melanie is close to her extended family as well. She has told no one in the family about her rape.

Melanie was reared in the Presbyterian Church, learning and loving biblical stories and favorite passages. At the beginning of high school, she "found her own faith." In the interview, she was quite comfortable using confessional language to explain the moral and faith-based ways she has tried to make sense of "the event."

"Hooking Up"

It was early in July after her junior year. Melanie lived in a summer sublet with a group of six college friends. They were holding a backyard barbecue that merged into a going-away party for one of the six. Around eight o'clock, friends began to show up. One of the guests was a "sophomore boy" who was interested in Melanie. Through the telling of her story, Melanie said she both was intrigued by this "cute boy" and wanted protection from him. Overall, she seemed nervous about his presence at the party. For two years, he had had a "forceful presence" and was very assertive about his attraction to her. They never dated.

Melanie wanted to "get the party going" because it was boring, so she led the crowd in a drinking game that she had learned from her days as a member of an intervarsity athletic team. Ten o'clock came and "the little sophomore boy" started to "hit on her," that is, whisper suggestive things into her ear. This made Melanie nervous. She knew she was drunk and he was aggressive; and although a house full of friends surrounded her, she was not sure that they could protect her from him.

Around half past ten, her ex-boyfriend showed up at the party. They had dated for three or four months the previous year, had a messy break-up, and then worked through it. She still considered him a friend. Melanie had had consensual sexual intercourse once in her life, and it was with this man when they were dating. On this evening, Melanie walked right up to him and, explaining that she was scared of this "little sophomore," said,

> I really just do not want him on top of me at all. . . . So
> I'm hanging onto you. I'm putting my arm in your arm
> and you're not letting this kid get near me.

Melanie assumed that her ex-boyfriend was not drunk and that he would keep her from harm.

> I knew I was pretty drunk and I really sort of saw my ex,
> to use a horrible word, as a savior figure, in the sense
> that "thank God he was there." All the rest of my
> friends were really drunk and they couldn't take care of
> me.

As the evening wore on, Melanie began to feel sick, so she asked her ex-boyfriend to take her upstairs to the bathroom, where she threw up several times. While she threw up, her ex-boyfriend was sitting on the stairs, hearing it all, and asking, "Dude, are you throwing up in there? Are you okay?" This point was important to Melanie because it proved to her that he knew she was drunk and not able to consent.

Despite her condition, she was happy to be away from the "sophomore boy." Throughout the evening, the focus of her concern was keeping away from him. After sitting on the stairs for a while, she asked her ex-boyfriend to take her to her room so that she could sleep it off.

Melanie was drunk enough that she does not clearly remember what happened next. What she does remember is that he put her in her bed and closed the door behind them. They started kissing and fondling.

> I really don't know how it happened, to be honest. I think
> we were both naked, and he ended up basically getting
> me in a corner, because the bed was in a corner. . . . And
> I think he sort of started to have sex with me without
> me really being aware. . . . Then, like, we must have had
> sex . . . except he didn't ejaculate; it was just entry . . . but
> like, for an extended period of time.

The next morning, a housemate asked Melanie about her evening. She denied that anything had happened. She was confused and in disbelief, so she went to her ex-boyfriend and asked him. Initially, he tried to laugh it off, but this confused her.

> I just sort of like, didn't say anything, but I immediately
> did not like that at all, because I mean you don't have
> sex with someone, especially when he knows that I was
> a virgin and then he knows that I haven't slept with any-
> one else. I was sort of in shock about his laughing it off,
> and I just wanted to get my own mind straight.

Melanie was confused and looking for clarification. Melanie spoke to this man two more times about it, each time confronting him with her take on the situation. A month later, he asked if they could "hook up" again. This angered Melanie.

Two days after the experience, Melanie told her housemate that she had "hooked up" with her ex-boyfriend, that it was really bad, and that it was a really upsetting experience. For the rest of the summer, these two women worked through her jumble of intense emotions. Through it all, the friend believed Melanie had had consensual sex.

The first person to understand the event as a rape was a classmate with whom Melanie shared interests in women's issues and religious matters. Melanie had not planned on telling her but decided that she was the perfect person to tell because she was trustworthy, interested in women's issues, and knew how Melanie felt about sexual intimacy.

Melanie has not told her family about the event. She does not know if she could ever tell them,

> not because I don't trust them with it. More because . . .
> I'm so afraid of hurting them . . . having them being
> emotionally wrecked about an experience that hap-
> pened to me. I wouldn't want to present it even though
> [not telling them] would hurt them.

Resisting Definitions
Melanie was not comfortable naming her experience as "rape." She knew that this research was about acquaintance rape (she sought me out), and she agreed to participate. Thus, at some

level, she saw her experience as rape. As with all the survivors, I asked Melanie what language she would like me to use as I talked about her experience of violation. Melanie did not want to put a label on it. A majority of her interview circled around this question. She had some suggestions about why she did not feel comfortable naming the experience. Her ambivalence and denial hinged on the question of her consent.

> The reason why I'm not comfortable with the word *rape* is probably a good deal about denial, and also because, while I didn't want it to happen, I wonder the extent to which I consented. I guess I'm not comfortable with the word because I'm not really comfortable with the idea. . . . I've never attached the word to it. So, until I really do things like this [interview] and talk to people, I don't want to put a label on something that I haven't really worked out in my head.

Throughout the interview, Melanie used the terms "really bad night," "what happened with him," "this experience," "sex," and "hooking up." As she talked about the evening and its aftermath, she verbally stumbled each time she approached a name for the experience. Often, she seemed to move haltingly toward "hooking up," which avoided labels and left it ambiguous. This reflected her own ambivalence about what really happened: sex or rape? When she eventually confided in two friends, she used "hooking up" to explain the rape. Even her friends seemed to be confused by the label. For almost a year after hearing of the event, they did not realize that the sex was both unwanted and, because of her intoxication, without consent. Only when Melanie clearly named it as unwanted did they understand.

Naming the actual details of the evening was difficult for Melanie. She was not clear what to call it because she was not sure what it was. The man put his penis in her vagina but did not ejaculate. She did not want that to happen and did not give consent. She was so drunk that she neither screamed nor said no.

So I don't know if that's the strict definition of rape [penis in the vagina without ejaculating], but to me, I mean, especially considering that I'd never do that, I define that as sex. I mean my own personal definition of sex is entry.[5]

Was this "real rape"? To Melanie, it seems to fit the definition of sex. She cannot make sense of it. She defines sex as "entry," and so if it was sex, how could it be rape?

"Physical Re-Livings"

Melanie strongly asserted that she did not have lasting physical effects from the rape. She says she is very comfortable with her body and has not felt any lasting symptoms. Once she was tested for a sexually transmitted disease and was sure she was not pregnant, she did not think much about her body's recovery. This stands in stark contrast to the fact that she has had "physical re-livings" (that is, flashbacks). These come at night and seem to be triggered when she thinks of other men. Because the flashbacks have been, according to Melanie, infrequent (once a month), she has not been very concerned about them. A year after the rape, she still has these "physical re-livings."

Incomprehensible Betrayal

For Melanie, sexual intimacy holds a moral, sacred, and relational quality. To misuse sex is a violation of all three. Sexual intimacy is so connected to sharing a part of herself with another that Melanie does not just "sleep around." Such belittling of sexual intimacy would be incomprehensible. Consequently, nonconsensual sex perpetrated by a friend would be an incomprehensible betrayal. Melanie once shared a part of herself with this man, and he, in turn, betrayed her. The betrayal was made that much more confusing because her ex-boyfriend knew how she felt about sex. He betrayed her standards.

> Physically, I think I'll get over it . . . but as far as, you
> know, my soul . . . I just can't imagine a world where
> someone like that could exist . . . who would have knowl-
> edge of me, would know me, would respect me. . . .
> That's the hardest thing. I mean, that you could just care
> so little for another human being.

This experience forced Melanie to examine who her friends really are and for whom she should and should not care. Melanie still cares a great deal about her ex-boyfriend. An intimacy was created when they shared a history of helping each other and divulging confidential details. Melanie does not understand how he could do this to her when he had shared private things with her, things that required trust.

> I mean, I can't imagine how he would trust me with the
> kind of information that he's trusted me with. . . . I don't
> understand how you could trust someone with stuff like
> that and then completely shatter them emotionally.
> Like fifteen minutes before, he should have thought
> that, you know, "I can't have sex with her because that
> might crush her."

Such betrayal by a trusted friend makes this experience that much more confusing for Melanie. Further, the betrayal was not simply physical. It was a betrayal of her soul.

> I think that when you have sex with someone you are
> really allowing them to have something intensely per-
> sonal, and it is something only you can give. . . . If I have
> sex with someone they better know. . . . I'll tell them
> that this means that I love them and this is not some-
> thing that I take lightly, and they have to appreciate
> that. He should have known that. I don't care how
> drunk he was; he knew that about me. And that's the
> hardest part, because I think that he betrayed more

than just getting in bed with me. My physical body can get over it; but he knew that was something important to my soul and who I was. That's what I'm going to have the hardest time dealing with as far as relating to him.

And betrayal brings on anger.

You know, man, it would be nice to be physically aggressive and just beat the living shit out of him. . . . Ah, that's not the answer either.

The pinpoint of her confusion and pain centered on her prior relationship with this man. The night of the "event," she had looked to him as her "savior" from the younger student she experienced as a predator. The man who raped her was the one to whom she "gave" her virginity the year before. For her, this history meant that the nonconsenting sexual intercourse had little to do with the act of sex and everything to do with betrayal and broken trust. For Melanie, the sin, and the focus of her struggle, was the broken relationship. Melanie was not interested in defining it as rape; it was betrayal.

Consent, Blame, and Alcohol

Although Melanie knew she felt betrayed, she had difficulty understanding the nature of the betrayal. Melanie was drunk when she asked her ex-boyfriend to help her to bed. Both Melanie and her ex-boyfriend were drunk when "it" happened. She is not clear about all of the details of the night. What she has pieced together is not very useful to her; it does not help her make sense of the betrayal. Melanie did not want to have sex that night. She told her ex-boyfriend that. He had sex with her anyway. Melanie believes that "it" happened only because she was drunk. She thus blames her use of alcohol for the violation. She recognizes that her boyfriend betrayed her trust, but she also blames herself for the rape.

The Importance of Believing in Herself

When asked what helped her cope in the aftermath of the rape, Melanie's immediate response was "denial." She went on to say that she has not really been "coping" as much as "dealing" or "figuring it out." Melanie's self-acceptance has helped her to deal with the rape.

> I think the idea that I really believe in myself physically and believe in myself mentally and emotionally is really important for me. I mean, the fact that no matter how bad this kid has treated me, he knows that I'm, you know, the best thing around town. . . . It will be hard for him to become as emotionally stable as me or whatever.

She finds solace in her own strength.

Unshakable Faith

Melanie uses confessional language to assert her firm connection to God. She has not felt that her faith in God has been harmed by this assault. After the rape, she started attending church more often "because it was a place of peace."

> I really believe that God is my rock and I can come to him in prayer. I feel very comfortable because he knows everything about the event, about how I felt at the time, how I feel now. He's universal. And that's just extremely comforting that I don't have to explain what happened and I don't have to explain how I feel because he just knows [in contrast to her friends]. . . . Prayer is very stabilizing, just because you don't have to feel ashamed or confused or muddled about it. It clears your thoughts—like taking a shower.

To Tell or Not to Tell

Melanie is ambivalent about talking about her experience. She is not convinced that telling people has any healing value.

> I think that if you keep talking to too many friends about it, you're changing the experience. You're making it sort of your mantra; you're making it sort of this cause. And all of your friends know you differently, and it's an emotional thing. That's really not a healing process. I think the healing process is you dealing with it personally and having a few people you can trust to add some resources.

A year after the rape, Melanie has told only two close friends. Despite her ambivalence, Melanie chose to tell me about the rape. She stated that her purpose in participating in this study was to benefit my research, other women, and religious professionals. Her desire to make a difference outweighed her need to protect her story.

Acquaintance rape is a sensitive topic to research. To attend to the health of all the participants, I included a set of assessment questions at the beginning of each interview. Questions about flashbacks, supportive networks, and medications were to serve the purpose of assessing whether the participant was in a safe enough place in her healing to participate in this study. I began Melanie's interview with these same assessment questions. Based on her responses, I proceeded with the interview. We both felt that she was able to talk safely about her experience.

Well into the interview, Melanie told me that I was not only the first professional she had told about the rape, but the first person to hear all the details. This information came up in the context of Melanie's explaining why she wanted a copy of the audio tape of her interview. (I gave all participants this option.)

> You know, that's the first time I've ever said . . . physically walking through the experience again . . . I think that's important to do when you are emotionally and mentally active and stable. . . . To be honest, the reason why I want this tape afterwards is for me personally. . . .

I doubt I will ever listen to it again. But physically having a tape, at least for me personally, is very comforting. You know, it makes the fact that these two hours are real. I can say this. I can do this. And I can hold on to it.

For Melanie, the interview was a way of beginning to confirm the realness of the rape. She has struggled with that. By voicing it aloud, she was claiming it as real. By having a copy of the audio tape, she would have "proof" that something happened. For Melanie, participating in this interview was an important part of her healing process. This was true, despite her previous disinterest in sharing her story with others.

Melanie's Suggestions for Religious Professionals
Initially, Melanie had a difficult time talking about what she thought clergy or other pastoral counselors should know or do for survivors of acquaintance rape. As she talked more about it, Melanie was able to articulate the qualities that a religious professional should have in order to work with survivors and what they should and should not do:
1. Listen, and do not talk more than the survivor.
2. Do not expound Bible references or biblical knowledge related to rape. Be a present resource, not an examiner of faith.
3. Be a person of faith:

> You need someone who you feel is of strong character and strong belief, and who believes that God will be there for you through this experience. . . . Any woman who comes to a clergyperson about a rape experience is going to be curious about faith and at least have some belief in the possibility of God. You know, why would you pick that person over your standard health services counselor? So, they're going to want to know how God relates to it.

4. Believe in her.

5. Stay in touch even though the trauma is not directly church-related.
6. Do not judge.
7. Let the survivor know you are willing to talk about it.
8. Be honest about your exposure to and knowledge about rape. Melanie thought this was important because it demonstrates that the authoritative clergyperson will not lord power over the woman. She thought it would be good to show some vulnerability by claiming how much you do and do not know.
9. Empathy is important, but there are limits to its helpfulness.

> I definitely want empathy, but I don't want so much empathy and sympathy to begin with that I would be drowning in emotions and I couldn't talk. . . . Sometimes if you get too emotional about it, you lose the ability to talk about it.

10. The gender of the minister matters. Melanie was clear that she would definitely not tell a male minister.

> I think that a clergywoman would understand how my body would physically feel through the "very penetrating experience." It's physically aggressive. It's attacking. And I don't think that a man would understand. . . . I think that a big part of it is being able to relate to clergy, so I think that many more women who are looking for resources would probably try to find a woman. . . . I would clearly go to a woman; there is no question about it.

Melanie's preference for telling a clergywoman does not reflect her desire to seek help from clergy in general. The minister of her home church and the minister of her college church are both women, and Melanie told neither of them.

Melanie was raped ten months before her interview with me. In that time, she has told two friends and me about the "experience." She is in a great amount of denial and confusion about what happened. Because she was drunk and because she is not sure if she consented, she does not know what to call the experience. She feels betrayed by a man who she thought understood her. This scenario seemed like her definition of accidental sex, and yet she does not have accidental sex. She had mutually consenting sex with this man once before. She did not want it this time. She is very conflicted because she still has feelings for this man. All this has left Melanie confused and unsure.

Abby

"I'm Not at Fault and It Was Rape"

Abby is a twenty-year-old, upper-middle-class white college sophomore from the Midwest. She is a member of a large United Methodist church at home, where they have had a pastoral change since she left for college. The first in her family to leave her geographic region for college, Abby is close to her parents, especially her dad, with whom she golfs whenever she is home. Abby told her parents about her rape shortly after it happened, and she feels both supported and burdened by their style of support. They are pleased that she is participating in this study.

Abby was raped at age nineteen at the end of her first year in college, after a party in which she was being initiated into the intervarsity golf team. Before the rape, Abby had not had sexual intercourse and considered herself "naive" when it came to men. After Abby was raped, she had a medical exam (but no rape kit) within forty-eight hours of the rape. The summer following the rape, she returned home and saw a (male) professional therapist. This was a good experience for her. Abby is a healthy, relaxed, and confident young adult.

"The Initiation"

Abby describes her evening, having to piece together parts of the story from others' accounts.

It was the night of my initiation for my golf team and they had given me way too many shots for what I could handle, and made me completely pass out . . . not pass out but have no memory after about nine o'clock at night. I was so drunk that they took me back to my room and took care of me in my room, and made sure that I wasn't going to die or anything. I was just passed out and fine in my room. They stayed with me for, I think it was, an hour in my room. And then they left. And a guy who had seen me earlier that night, and knew how drunk I was, and knew what state I was in, let himself into the dorm room and into my room and had sex with me while I was passed out in my bed, I guess. I woke up the next morning . . . because I never had sex before; there was blood all over the sheets and I felt very sore. It was pretty scary when I woke up and I didn't really know what had happened. So, I talked to a girl on my golf team, and she said, "We have to go to the doctor." So we went to the [University Department of Health] and they said that I had been raped.

The Power of Naming It Rape

Abby did not want to report the rape, or even have the doctors examine her.

> Basically, I didn't want to go, because I felt like I knew pretty much what had happened, and that, given the situation, at that point, I didn't define it as rape at all. So I was just like, "I guess I had sex with somebody" and that's it. And my friend Trish was like, "No, Abby, you have to go and get them to check this and tell you what happened." So I went with her. I didn't really want to go very much at all, but just with her being like, "You really should go." . . . It was not my idea to go at all. . . . I just wanted to forget that it had happened and not talk about it with anyone because I didn't define it as rape at all at that point.

At first, Abby did not define it as rape. She blacked out before the rape and still has no memory of it. (Witnesses later identified the rapist.) It was not until after the staff at the health center, a friend, her parents, her counselor, and literature named it as such that she began to understand and claim it is as rape:

> I think I didn't accept it as rape until the summer after when I was talking to my counselor. My parents obviously were just like, "Abby, you have to talk to somebody." They defined it as rape from the beginning. But I definitely didn't. My counselor gave me books to read about it and stuff and just seeing other reports of it—and them defining it as rape and I was like, "Oh, this does happen to other people and this is a situation that does occur and it is rape." I guess it was talking to the counselor and having him just being like, "You know, you couldn't have done anything and it's not your fault at all." Him making it clear to me and then reading it, definitely. The combination of those. I kinda needed other people's confirmation of it, definitely, besides my own. . . . It took me a long time to figure out that it wasn't me at all.

Naming the experience as rape was an important step in Abby's healing; naming it as rape and asserting that it was not her fault went hand in hand. Having multiple confirmations of this naming was crucial to Abby's healing process. Over and over, hearing that it was rape, and that it was not her fault, eventually brought her to believe and accept it.

Naming the trauma as rape was difficult, in part, because Abby knew the man who raped her. Knowing the perpetrator also made it hard for her to name it as a crime.

> I was really good friends with this guy before it happened, and so it was just because I know him it's hard to be like, "You raped me." I know him so well.

Knowing the rapist also contributed to her reluctance to seek medical attention and her unwillingness to report the rape to the police.

Confusion and Lack of Control

Immediately after the rape, Abby felt a combination of confusion and lack of control. Because she was passed out when she was raped, the rape was even more confusing.

> I was just feeling completely out of it. You're just like, "What's going on?" Like, "What happened?". . . especially for me, since I had no idea what had happened. I still was just like, "Ahhh! What was this?". . . In the beginning, you're just very, very confused . . . I didn't know what had happened. Confused is a good word, I think; confused. I lost a lot of control and had no idea what the rape was.

Immediately after the rape, Abby felt out of control and scared. Friends and family exacerbated this fear by telling her what she "needed" to do. Abby sees both the positives and the negatives of her support system's response.

> It was just really scary to have people tell me what to do. And that is something I definitely want to make clear: You have to be able to decide what you want to do yourself. I think even a pastor might be more apt to be like, "You have to report this." But they really shouldn't because it makes it a lot harder.
>
> By the time I got to the doctors, it was more than twenty-four hours after it had happened so they couldn't really do the rape kit then. At that point, I don't think that I would have wanted them to use the rape kit because I definitely was not defining it as rape. . . . I was just going to the hospital because my friend was like, "You need to do this." In the long run, it was very good that she made me do that, or else I would not have

thought about it at all or dealt with it at all. So, it was lucky that she had me go in there.

Telling her parents added to Abby's confusion.

> When I got home and told my parents, they of course, you know, they had no idea what to do. So they just were really upset and my dad was like, "I'm going to fly out to the kid's home and I'm going to shoot him." Him being a good friend of mine, I was like, "No." At this point, I didn't define it as rape, so I was just like, "Oh, my God." And my dad was like, "You have to report it. You have to call the police. I'm calling the police no matter if you want to or not. We're reporting this and we have to get something done about this." And I was just like, "Ahhh!" It just made it so much worse for me. . . .
>
> To an extent it was kind of nice to know that they cared so much about me that they did just want to go blow the kid's head off. But that also was really scary at that point. So it was really nice to have their support. Of course, they did support me so much. They just didn't know how to show it. It would have been better if they had been like, "We hate him and we love you so much, but you're in control. If you want to do this, you can."

In the end, Abby could see her parents' effort as supportive, although misdirected. When asked what she would say to a rape victim, Abby was clear that giving her back some control was crucial.

> I'd tell her, "First of all, you don't have to do anything. There's nothing that is prescribed for you to do. You don't have to tell anybody. You don't have to report this to anybody. You can if you want to, and it's good if you want to. But you are in control." A lot of it is a control issue. Tell her, "We're here for you, and we love you, and you can talk to us whenever you need to." It's helpful

just to have people around you. The most important thing to say is, "You can do whatever you want to do." That was the most important thing for me.

Long-Term Healing

Initially, Abby blamed herself for the rape. Working with a counselor was crucial for her because through him, she grew to understand that it was not her fault and, at the moment of the rape, she could have done nothing to stop it. Coming to understand this was not an easy thing for Abby. Even the knowledge that she was passed out during the rape did not make this understanding any easier. A year after the rape, Abby is still very in touch with those feelings of self-blame, although cognitively she knows she did nothing wrong. Several times during the interview Abby explained the healing power of understanding her lack of culpability.

> I felt basically like, "Why did I do that?" Because I still felt, like, at fault, and then it took me a while to be like, "Listen, I couldn't have done anything differently than I had done. . . . I couldn't have done anything because I was passed out and was not capable of doing anything."
>
> From my point of view the most important thing for a clergyperson to do is being able to say, "You couldn't have done anything; it was not your fault." For me, defining it as rape was important. And I can see that as an issue for most acquaintance rapes. Just actually defining it as rape is very hard. It's not very easy because it isn't your textbook guy jumping out of a bush. It's much harder to define. So I think for a pastor to be able to sit down and be like, "This has happened to other people, he did rape you, it's not your fault." And just being so much more knowledgeable about it.

Grieving the Loss of Normalcy

In addition to her early feelings of culpability, Abby did not feel "normal" after the rape, a feeling she desperately missed. She did not want to have a medical check-up because she did not want to see herself as anything but the same old Abby. She missed this person.

> I didn't feel like a normal person. It takes a while, but just talking to people and having them be there for you puts you back with them, I guess. . . . You don't feel like the same person at all . . . you just want to be the same person you were before, but you know that you aren't. And it's hard to realize that you're not the same person, but you're not a worse person because of it.

After the rape, Abby felt alone, vulnerable, and separated. Being raped meant a loss of feeling part of the community. Initially, she told only one friend. Even after she told more friends, she felt as though this "unusual experience" made her an "other."

> I think you feel, to an extent, by yourself. Nobody else [her friends] had to deal with this before and didn't have a lot to say personally. So I was just kind of like, me by myself over here and there was everybody else over there.

Abby's story is filled with signs of her own healing. It started with naming it rape and recognizing that she was not at fault. This happened because she had a supportive group of family and friends and a good counselor who remained committed, even faithful, to her. Having worked out some issues, Abby decided that her next step in claiming "normalcy" was to talk to the man who raped her.[6] Abby knew that she would have to see this man daily, and so she decided that she did not want to hide from him. As she stated, not confronting him would be worse. The goal then, in this confrontation, was not to elicit an apology from him, or even draw out a confession of guilt, but to tell him how it had affected her and how she felt.

I actually talked to him about it when I came back to school in the fall. I had to. I was going nuts; I had to talk to him. I don't think his intention was to hurt me like he did. But nevertheless, he did. And I was just like, "Listen, you raped me. You did hurt me whether you intended to hurt me or not. You did and this is how I feel. I need to let you know how I feel." And he was very defensive, actually. He was just like, "Listen, I don't know what you think, but. . . ." I don't think he defines it as rape at all. But it was definitely just helpful to me. . . I had to just say something to him. And just let him know that I feel like he did this to me.

Abby found that reading firsthand accounts of survivors was also important in helping her name her experience as rape. It helped her place her experience within a context and within a group of people. Reading firsthand accounts helped her normalize her experience and, in turn, feel less alone. The accounts became a reality check; she was not such an outsider after all.

I've definitely read a lot about [rape] and found it very helpful. Especially in just defining it, and reading that it happened to other people; I do think you feel very much alone. Just reading about it is helpful. That was actually not something that my counselor recommended. I did that on my own. . . . I don't necessarily think the advice from the books was all that helpful because it's a lot harder to take advice if you're just reading it. But I think just the accounts of it, and knowing that it did happen to other people . . . and that my specific situation wasn't so weird.

Personal Strength and Self-Care
Knowing that she has survived the experience has made Abby stronger than she thought possible. When asked what helps her cope now, Abby responded,

> I think just knowing for myself that I've gone through it
> and I'm fine. I'm basically the same person that I was
> before and I have all my friends around me who know
> about it and are there for me—no matter what. I think
> that's probably the most important thing for me. . . . I
> think there is also the sense, though, that having gone
> through it, you feel like you can go through more than
> you thought and you're a stronger person. . . . For me,
> it's kind of nice. I always think of myself as little Abby
> from a small town, and kind of naive. Or I used to, and
> then after this I guess it's not so much. I feel, like, more
> empowered to an extent. . . . It's better to be like that, I
> guess, than so scared.

Allowing her community of friends to help her has played an important part in Abby's ongoing process of healing. She now invites her friends, from whom she initially concealed the rape, to participate in her own self-care.

> I always make sure there is somebody around me who
> knows what happened. I make sure I'm not in a situa-
> tion where I have to deal with it myself. That's pretty
> important. . . . Also, within the power that I have, just
> making sure that I am safe and knowing what's going on,
> to the extent that I can control things.

Abby knows that she cannot be in complete control of every situation, but she does have the power to make choices that help her feel safe. Knowing that she has power has been crucial to her healing.

Men and the Limits of Support

Abby was pleased with the therapist she found and indicated that his gender made no difference. With friends, however, Abby suggested there was a difference. Abby felt supported by her current boyfriend but felt that he and other men had a difficult time dealing with the rape.

I think it's harder for my guy friends to deal with. I've only told a few guys and, of course, I told my boyfriend. It's even harder for them because they know the guy who did it and they liked him and they'd probably say that they still do like him. So, it's harder from a guy's standpoint to understand. Where girls are just like, "Oh, we feel so badly for you" because they can empathize with that. For my boyfriend, I think he feels really badly for me, but also he doesn't like to deal with it very much. He'd rather not deal with it.

The Interview as a Way to Make a Difference

Abby was eager to participate in this study; in fact, she initiated the contact. It was a way for her to make a positive difference in the life of other women.

> I feel like if something really bad like this happens, any positive thing that can come from it is really good. And that's why I'm doing this interview . . . so that people who have been through it can get more help. I know it just ruins them, and I can definitely see how that would happen. But hopefully, they'll be able to deal with it a little better. And clergy, I guess, will be better able to help them if they know more about it. So I feel like if I can do that, that's good.

It was important to Abby that good have the last word. When asked if she wanted to add anything to the interview, Abby named two things. The first had to do with her own healing. After the rape, Abby felt alone, confused, scared, at fault, and empty. It has been a year since the rape, and she feels much stronger and more aware. She is still trying to "figure things out," but she is grateful to note her growth and healing. During the interview, Abby asked me two questions: "Is my case typical?" and "Does this happen to other women?" She was relieved to hear that her situation of party-alcohol-rape is not statistically unusual and that it is highly likely that some women she knows have been raped. Knowing the unsettling facts about acquaintance rape has helped Abby put her own healing into a broader context and made her feel less isolated.

The second issue concerned her parents. Abby's parents are angry with the rapist and concerned for her. They have not talked to anyone about their feelings. Abby wishes her parents would talk to their minister about it. She believes it would help them.

Abby's Suggestions for Religious Professionals

Abby had many supportive persons around her immediately after the rape and over a longer time frame. All of them helped in her healing. From the friend who took her to get a medical check-up, to her parents, to her counselor, all worked together to help her face the reality of the rape. From her experiences with these people, Abby lifted up several things religious professionals should know and do for a survivor immediately after the rape and in the long-term:

1. Listen and help her understand that it was not her fault.
2. Name it as rape.
   She named these two as the most important tasks for religious professionals.
3. Having a survivor read firsthand accounts by other survivors can be very helpful.
4. Do not make decisions for her; give her options. It is scary to have people tell you what to do. A survivor does not have to do anything if she does not want to. It is important to give her back control. A pastor is more likely to tell her to report it. That makes it harder.
5. Do not threaten to retaliate against the attacker.
6. Feelings related to the rape do not always occur during office hours. Friends and clergy can be supportive of her by being present as much as possible.
7. A woman does not need to try to deal with it by herself.
8. Attend to the needs of parents and family members.

Abby was raped a year ago and has been able to name it as rape, believe that it was not her fault, tell friends and family, seek out therapeutic help, and reach out to help others. In short, Abby has done an amazing job of attending to her own healing process. In doing so, she has not only survived the rape but found good out of the bad.

Survivors of acquaintance rape have a wealth of information to share with religious professionals about what can help them recover. The women in this study agree that listening, affirming, and believing are imperative. They also agree that the community plays an important role, although they disagree on the limits of its helpfulness. Themes such as self-blame, loss, naming the violence, and lack of control appeared in each of their narratives. One woman found that forgiveness was important. Two used their experiences as a litmus test for future relationships. All of the women offered helpful comments for religious professionals. Putting the stories together, we begin to see a list of similar and complementary psychospiritual themes emerging. These themes suggest the possibility of a pastoral theological framework for understanding a survivor's experience. We now turn to this framework.

4.

A Pastoral Theological Framework

Forty-five years of psychosocial research has provided a wealth of information on acquaintance rape.[1] This research has generated many crucial psychosocial and sociohistorical theories about survivors' experiences. These theories, however, do not attend to the psychospiritual implications of acquaintance rape. My goal in this work is to provide a pastoral theological framework to understand acquaintance rape and pastoral guidelines for working with acquaintance rape survivors.

In chapter 3, we listened to four distinct accounts of acquaintance rape. Viewed together, these stories produce several common pastoral theological themes. Some of these themes take on traditional theological forms and language. More often, these profound psychospiritual matters appear in everyday, even mundane, relational language. What defines these themes as theological is not their overt connection to God, Jesus, or the church, but their fundamental connection to a survivor's ability to live, thrive, and make meaning in her world.

Several pastoral theological themes emerge from the experiences of these four survivors. This list is not exhaustive, nor is it applicable to every survivor's struggle. Rather, these themes begin to present a pastoral theological framework for understanding an acquaintance rape survivor's experience of trauma and healing.

World-Shattering

Acquaintance rape is the violation of a woman's bodily integrity, relational integrity, psychospiritual and sexual integrity, and the incarnate Spirit of God within her. It can shatter her way of being in the world. Following a rape, a woman's ability to block out thoughts of violence is devastated by the violence itself. Nonconsensual, forced, sexualized violence invades a woman both physically and psychospiritually. This shattering is obvious in bruises, blood, and physical trauma. It also means that her emotional and spiritual health has been bruised, broken, torn; it leaves her in tremendous pain. When a woman is raped, she experiences not only a physical violation of her sacred body but a violation and shattering of her psychospiritual world.

Rape is a crime resulting in psychospiritual losses. Much more than an invasion of our "private parts," it violates a woman's body at the site of procreation, birth, and sexual ecstasy.[2] Christian tradition and theology are infused with, and reinforce, notions of the mind/body split, denying the sacredness of the body. Experientially, however, we somatically know that our bodily integrity represents the boundaries of the Self. The assault of those most private parts of our bodies is a violation of our very psychospiritual core. More than a loss of physical integrity, rape can lead to the spiritual losses of trust, faith, innocence, hope, meaning, joy, future, and intimacy.[3] Acquaintance rape can shatter a woman's psychospiritual holding environment.

The idea of a cognitive and psychospiritual holding environment is not new. Jean Piaget saw it in terms of psychic equilibrium.[4] When trauma is encountered, disequilibrium occurs. Defense mechanisms help us equalize the trauma. We live in trauma until we can reorganize, classify, and make sense of it. When it is not resolved sufficiently in our psyche, it is manifest in pathology.

Psychodynamically, the shattering is a loss of homeostasis or systemic balance. During a crisis event, homeostasis is interrupted and homeostatic mechanisms do not work. Solutions previously learned to solve problems no longer function, do not apply, and therefore cannot be used to return to homeostasis. This failure of known or attempted solutions results in personal disorganization. Further, during a crisis, individuals are more susceptible to sociocultural influences from the environment. They have lost their ability to prioritize the value of these influences and thus can experience an increased feeling of vulnerability.

A psychosocial paradigm presents acquaintance rape in a relational way. It does not, however, offer a way in which to see how the relational aspects of the violence affect a woman's soul. In a psychospiritual framework, as we shall see, acquaintance rape is experienced as betrayal, creating problems in naming, self-blame, desecration of the body, loss of normalcy, and loss of community.

Betrayal and the Loss of Eden

Betrayal is the dominant traumatic psychospiritual issue for survivors of acquaintance rape. This betrayal stems from the brokenness caused by the very act of violence. It emerges out of a relationship that originally involved the existence of a level of trust. This level of trust allows the man to have access to the woman in the first place, and trust can move the woman to suspend any intuitive voice of caution. Because trust is a definitional factor in the relationship, betrayed trust is an unavoidable outcome. In stranger rape, fear of death and harm dominate a survivor's recovery.[5] With acquaintance rape, the survivor struggles with the loss of trust and incomprehensible betrayal.

Melanie experienced rape by her ex-boyfriend as an enormous betrayal. She knew it was a violation. She was not ready to give it a name, but she was clear that it was a broken trust and an incomprehensible betrayal. At the center of her pain and confusion was the betrayal of her moral, relational, physical, and religious standards. This man had known her. She had shared with him the core matters of her being. She had told him that sexual intimacy was a matter for serious moral and religious consideration. Yet he raped her. He did not just contradict her; he betrayed her. For Melanie, the betrayal made no sense. As she attempted to comprehend her experience, it was easier and psychospiritually safer to believe that he was too drunk to know better. To believe that he was sober and thus able to negate her will and forgo her consent would mean either seeing him in a new light (which would mean she was a bad judge of character) or facing a dangerous theodicy. Believing that he meant to rape her would mean recognizing that (1) bad things do happen to good people, and (2) they happen for no justifiable reason. To accept this is to accept that sometimes chaos and evil reign. For Melanie, believing that the rapist chose to violate and betray her just because he could, would mean giving up the notion that humans are fundamentally good and do good. Believing that he was too drunk to know better was Melanie's way of protecting her worldview. Intentional evil is much more devastating than evil by accident.

Ronnie Janoff-Bulman addresses this notion of trauma and recovery with her just-world theory. A just-world theory asserts that human beings want to assume that we live in an orderly world and that we can expect to be protected from misfortune. The internal dialogue sounds like this:

> My world is benevolent. Even in such a good world negative events happen, even if relatively infrequently. Yet, when they occur they are not random, but rather meaningfully distributed. They happen to people who deserve them, either because of who they are or what they did or failed to do. I am a good, competent, careful person. Bad things couldn't happen to me.[6]

Inherent in this mind-set is an "illusion of invulnerability" in which we overestimate the likelihood of positive events and underestimate the likelihood of negative events. When bad things do happen to us or to someone else, our initial response is to try to fit them into this present just-world theory. It is easier to believe in a just or benevolent world (even though we have no evidence for it) than it is to accept reality and lose paradise.

Likewise, in her work on violence against children, Alice Miller suggests that society lives in deep denial. We are prone to denial because we "prefer to take upon ourselves the hell of blindness, alienation, abuse, deception, subordination, and loss of self rather than lose that place called paradise, which offers us security."[7] We are in denial about the realities of acquaintance rape because we have an investment in protecting our sense that things happen for a reason. We are lured by the temptation of disbelief. Giving up the illusion that bad things only happen to bad people is costly. If bad things can happen to good people, then bad things could happen to me. If bad things can happen to me for no reason, then I am in danger, and chaos rules. Accepting the possibilities and realities of acquaintance rape means giving up Eden.

For the survivors in this study, betrayal was at the heart of their struggle to make sense of the violence. They named their betrayal in religious terms. For Hannah, the stolen crucifix off her wall was a metaphor for the enormity of the losses she had experienced. "He got God, too" became a lament for her tremendous loss. God did not abandon her. God was stolen, along with her identity, her safety, her self-confidence, and more. For Debra, God was not there during the rape because "God don't like ugly." God was not abandoning her in the rape because God was just not present. Debra did not expect God to be there because she knew God did not approve. God's absence was God's judgment; this made Debra angry. For Melanie, betrayal came from the man she considered her "savior figure." The evening she was raped, Melanie was wary of unwanted sexualized advances by a man at the party. She went to her ex-boyfriend, her "savior," because she saw him as safe enough and sober enough to protect her. Her savior betrayed her by raping her. This betrayal left Melanie confused, sad, and angry.

The pastoral theological literature on sexualized violence suggests that survivors can feel abandoned by God. This is articulated in questions about the cause and purpose of suffering.[8] These women did not directly name abandonment by God as a central feature of their trauma. But they did name betrayal, the most pronounced issue for three of the four survivors, in theological ways. Betrayal is not just a human foible but a violation of the soul.

The betrayal these women felt was profound, much more than a broken promise or voiced secret. It took on divine proportions. For three of the women, their suffering directly affected their own notions of God's power. Hannah's lament for a stolen crucifix was her lament in the face of a power so big that it could even steal God. Hannah was betrayed by a god not big enough to stand strong in the face of evil. If God could not endure it, then how could she? God did not cause the suffering, but neither could God stop it. After the rape, Hannah felt she could not endure empty platitudes about the love of God because God had already been proven to be anything but steadfast. As Marie Fortune suggests, Hannah made a connection between her suffering and God's power, or in this case, the lack thereof.[9] Hannah saw her suffering neither as a sign of God's disfavor nor as a sign that God does not play by the rules. But her suffering occurred while God was overpowered. N. Duncan Sinclair suggests that this struggle reflects one's inability to believe that there can be anything greater than that which inflicted the pain.[10]

Debra, on the other hand, did experience her suffering as a sign of God's disfavor. Her loneliness in suffering was not so much a passive abandonment by God as a direct judgment by God. In this complete disapproval, God was not distinguishing between violator and violated. For Debra, this overall judgment left her no way to distinguish between the evil done and her inability to stop it. Evil was done to her, and therefore she was evil. Debra's question of theodicy ("Why did God let this happen to me?") was immediately answered with God's judgment ("Because God don't like ugly"). As Debra struggled to heal her dislocation, anger, and loss caused by the violence, she had to heal her concept of a powerfully judging God. Marie Fortune reminds us that such a healing process, often expressed through anger at religious professionals, religious communities, and God (as in Debra's case) can be a sign that they have not given up on God or God's representatives.[11]

Melanie's betrayal came at the hands of her "savior." Putting her trust in him set her up for an even bigger descent into hell. Melanie did not use confessional language to express her sorrow, but her suffering took on such absolute power that only theological imagery could adequately describe her experience.

Wrestling for a Name

Naming and being named are sacred activities in the Judeo-Christian tradition. To be named is to be known; to name is to claim power. Jacob wrestled with the messenger who had no name (Gen. 32:24-30). In the end, Jacob came away with a blessing. For survivors of acquaintance rape, naming the experience is crucial to their healing process. This naming process is often a wrestling match, with the wrestling partners being self-blame and the question of consent. A year after Melanie's "experience," she was not sure what to call it. She knew it was wrong; she knew it was not accidental sex; she knew she did not want it while it was happening; and she knew she felt betrayed. During her interview, she continued to wrestle for a name. She was not eager for me or others to name it, and yet she wrestled—alone. She had been drunk and she did not say no. She was not sure if that meant she consented. A year after the rape, Melanie is still wrestling for a name. Until she comes away with its name, Melanie will be unable to claim a healing blessing.

Abby knew the name was rape, and she knew it was not her fault. This naming process did not happen all at once or in isolation. Initially, she did not want to get medical attention because she believed it was an insignificant matter. It was only with a chorus of committed family, friends, a therapist, doctors, and other survivors' stories that she could name her experience acquaintance rape. Abby has no conscious memory of the rape because she was passed out during it. Even so, she had to wrestle with self-blame and consent. It was only after many people joined her in the wrestling match that she could grab the concept and literally "come to terms" with the rape. Naming is an ongoing process for acquaintance rape survivors because self-blame and guilt are ongoing adversaries.

Knowing the acquaintance rapist makes the naming process very difficult. It makes no sense that someone you know and trust would do such evil. This cognitive dissonance can therefore hinder the naming process. Even after naming the experience "rape," survivors can have a difficult time calling the perpetrator a rapist. None of the women in this study named the violators "rapists." Even Hannah, whose successful court case declared that he was a rapist, could not use his newly assigned title: Violator? Perpetrator? Bad Man? Yes. Rapist? No. Having a previous relationship with an acquaintance rapist renders the name-wrestling difficult and adds another dimension to a woman's struggle to heal.

"Real Rape" and the Myth of the Virgin Mary Survivor
The naming process does not end with the survivor. In fact, the survivor's struggle to name the violence is enveloped by the wider society's confusion over what constitutes "real rape." Unfortunately, concepts of real rape are defined by a compilation of all the classic rape myths. Melanie could not believe that her experience was rape because it did not fit the public image of rape. This was not an image that she actively created; it was handed to her by society. The definition of a "real rape," that is, one that is completely believable, adheres to a scenario that is pure and holy. A "real rape" survivor takes on a Virgin Mary quality.

The scenario might look like this: Mary is surprised by a stranger who has a gun or a knife. She fights back enough so that the bruises and cuts show. She yells "no" but is raped. She immediately calls the police and gets an escort to the hospital, where they are equipped to collect evidence in a caring and thorough way. There are enough visible cuts, bruises, blood, saliva, semen, and pieces of the assailant's clothing to corroborate her story. She has had no mind-altering food, drug, or drink. She is a virgin or at least has a stellar enough reputation that she has not had sex with this man before. (This is, of course, because she is a good judge of character.) She is a virgin, not because she has not had opportunities for sex but because she has made the choice to wait until marriage. In other words, she is not desperate for sex. She is not too quiet. Neither is she too aggressive, loud, or rambunctious because that would imply that she had it coming. She wears nonseductive clothing: nothing tight, clingy, low cut, or anything that could draw attention to her body—in other words, nothing in style. She is not too friendly with men because she might be seen as coming on to them, but she has a "good reputation" (which of course could mean anything). She is not too "churchy" because that would mean she is sexually repressed and would charge rape after consensual sex because she felt guilty. It would be best if she were protecting her children at the time of the rape because that is the sign of a good woman.

Of course, even if the rape is real, her response to it also determines the reality of the rape. If she suffers publicly, she is hysterical. If she suffers too quietly, then it could not really have been violence. If she suffers too long, she is mentally unstable or defensive, or paranoid, or just completely irrational. (She just needs to move on!) She is at all times a clear, rational, and forgiving thinker. If she is too angry, she is a man-hater. If she is virtuous enough, she will forgive him because he is mentally incapable of knowing he has done something wrong, or he was abused as a child, or he is an alcoholic, or he is disempowered by the system, or because she is a Christian and by forgiving him she can love him to repentance. She then volunteers to work in the prisons, not with women who killed their abusers (they are mentally unstable and angry), but with the rapists and abusers who have been forgotten by society and yet deserve another chance because she is called to hate the sin but love the sinner.

A bit extreme. But the point is, this Virgin Mary survivor does not exist. Because of the myth of real rape, there is no such thing as a completely believed acquaintance rape survivor. Well over half of all rapes are committed by someone known to the victim, most do not involve a weapon, most do not involve injury beyond minor bruises or scratches, and most occur indoors in either the victim's or assailant's home. Too often we look at a situation of rape, compare its veracity to this Virgin Mary scenario, and judge it accordingly. Virgin Mary survivors and "real rapes" (that is, those that fit our myth if not our statistics) are the standards of rape for many people, including law enforcement, medical personnel, family, friends, and the church. Unrealistic standards such as these keep women from naming their experiences as rape.

Consent and the Myth of Mary the Temple Prostitute

The myth of the Virgin Mary survivor is a strong force because it creates a nonexistent and harmful archetype of an acquaintance rape survivor. At the heart of the problem is the matter of consent: What did this woman do to cause or at least invite such violence? What does it say about a woman who asked for such mistreatment? We move from the Virgin Mary survivor to Mary the Temple Prostitute. Rape by an acquaintance falls outside the parameters of "real rape." If the action was not rape, the woman reasons, she must have asked for it. And only a shameful woman asks for such treatment. When consent is at the heart of the struggle for healing, a survivor can feel like Mary the Temple Prostitute.

All the women in this study struggled with the question of consent and blame. They blamed themselves for their rapes.

Debra believed that she caused the second rape because she had not loudly protested the first rape. Melanie and Abby reasoned that although their alcohol intake made them unable to give consent, they consented to the alcohol itself and so must somehow have consented to all the actions that followed. Confusing their vulnerability with their responsibility, they confessed consent. In this scenario, lack of nonconsent emerges as consent. When consent is murky, *no* can mean anything. In the words of a victim,

> I had fully internalized the view that a woman is somehow to blame if she is raped. . . .
>
> Although I held him ultimately responsible, I couldn't help scrutinizing my own behavior. I had consented to everything up until that point. I knew what my limits were, but it's possible I didn't make myself clear to him. Maybe the word no wasn't enough.[12]

Questions of consent emerge as feelings of shame and guilt. Some have suggested that this guilt and shame are "misdirected" when they stem from the inappropriate claim of consent. Although guilt and shame might be ill-founded, they are natural responses to confusion about consent. Indeed, because guilt is so socially conditioned, survivors have to be countercultural to avoid these feelings. Religious professionals working with survivors therefore need to distinguish between a survivor's struggle with culpability and "misdirected" or erroneous guilt. In confusing self-blame and consent, we pathologize guilt and hold the survivor responsible for inculturated guilt and shame.

The question of consent is crucial to a survivor's struggle, in part because it represents the larger question about the difference between sexual activity and sexualized violence.[13] Consent in this context is the informed and freely chosen agreement to engage in sexual activity. Distinguishable from submission or the yielding to the power of another, consent requires that a person have all the necessary information to make a decision, the power to choose, and the integrity to be respected for that decision. In rape, there is no consent; rape is a violation of a relationship. Legal definitions of rape hinge on this matter of consent.[14]

Where there is unequal or coercive power (as opposed to persuasive) power, there is no consent.[15] In rape, the mechanics (the physical instruments of rape) might be sexual, but the primary motivation is not. To go against a woman's will is to act without her consent. To act without consent is a crime. This principle of consent can serve as the guide for differentiating between coercive sex and consensual sex, that is, between sexualized violence and sexual activity.

As long as we see rape as an extreme expression of sexual activity, we will confuse sexual activity with sexualized violence. Fortune asserts that to distinguish between the two, we need to take seriously this notion of consent. Sexual activity is, by definition, consensual and takes place in a context of mutuality, respect, equality, caring, and responsibility. Sexualized violence is, by definition, nonconsensual and takes place in the context of exploitation, hostility, and abuse.[16]

Women have been socialized to doubt their own experiences. Nowhere is this more true than when an acquaintance rape survivor questions her own culpability for being violated. Survivors, however, are not alone in this blaming activity. Even the best-intentioned care provider can ask "consensual questions." Consensual questions are those inquiries that search for clarity in the violence: What were you wearing? Why didn't you scream? Were you drinking?—anything that makes the violence logical. Such questions are directed toward finding logic in the violence. It is a search for order in the chaos. As a pastoral care matter, when we ask a survivor too many details about the rape, we run the risk of asking consensual questions and leaving her feeling that we do not believe her.

Consensual questions may help us find logic in the acquaintance rape, but I suggest that they are also unconscious attempts to create distance from the manifestation of the chaos itself—the rape. In asking consensual questions, caring persons leave the role of believer and enter the role of adjudicator and self-preservationist. If we can make sense of the situation and if we can decipher what a victim did to bring on the violence, we can satisfy our own terror by concluding that the victim is different from us. Difference, in this case, is safer. If the victim is different, that is, if the victim did some identifiable action that brought on the violence, then we, by avoiding that behavior, can avoid the violence. But if my behavior is not different enough from the survivor's, then I, too, am vulnerable to the violence. I am no longer safe. By asking the blatant (What did you do to cause the rape?) and the hidden (Were you drinking?) consensual questions, we not only live in the fantasy that our behavior will never put us at risk but blame her for the rape and distance ourselves from her. Consensual questions can leave the survivor feeling lonely and reinforce her own self-blaming attitudes.

Religious professionals can help survivors of acquaintance rape by taking care to avoid consensual questions and reassuring them that they did nothing to bring on the rape. Abby could move on with her healing only after she had help claiming that she neither invited the rape nor could have stopped it once she passed out. Survivors need to take no responsibility for the violence. Because victim-blaming is so consistently present, victims/survivors need to hear that people *will* blame them. This does not mean that they are to blame. Survivors need fair warning about these realities, not platitudes or empty assurances.

The Body as the Desecrated Scene of the Crime

Acquaintance rape usually occurs in familiar locations. This was true for all the women in this study. Because acquaintance rape violates a woman's notion of "safe space," an important element of her healing process must include a reclaiming of the location of the crime. In doing so, the survivor can live a life with fewer fears of the memories. This can be painfully difficult after an acquaintance rape because her body is the holding place of memories. For survivors of acquaintance rape, the body is the desecrated scene of the crime.

With any violence, the location of the crime is important. Extensive legal knowledge is not required to know that yellow tape around an area signals a recent crime. The crime tape is the sign to stay away and leave the questions to the experts. For a survivor of acquaintance rape, the primary scene of the crime is not a house address but her body. This becomes clear when a woman goes to a hospital for a medical investigation and use of the rape kit. When the rape kit is used, the woman's body as scene of the crime is photographed, combed, plucked, and searched for evidence of the offender and the offense. In this medical exam, the woman is checked for physical damage and proof of the violation. If she is not hurt enough, if the scene of the crime does not display enough evidence, she may not be believed.

This medical examination and the police inquiry following a rape can add to the survivor's feeling of desecration, invasion, and loss of privacy. When a victim reports a rape to the police and agrees to go to the hospital for a medical exam, she will go through a basic medical check and the "rape kit." The rape kit is the process by which medical personnel representing the legal system collect evidence of the rape from the victim's body, checking for scrapes, cuts, blood, semen, skin under the fingernails, and any evidence that might verify the violence. If the survivor presses charges, the rape kit is crucial. Going through the rape kit can feel like a reinvasion. The invasive nature of the exam adds to the present feeling of loss of privacy. In addition, victims, despite their age, do not always know the names of body parts and functions and may be too embarrassed to ask. I learned this one night from a young girl. In the hospital trauma room, the police officers were using specific anatomical language as they asked her about the details of her rape. Because she was a "streetwise" tough talker, the officers took her short and "unhelpful" responses as indications of her worldliness. In the middle of the questioning, I, the rape advocate, asked the young girl, "When they say 'vagina,' do you know what part of your body they are talking about?" Quietly she responded, "No." She was ashamed of being raped and she was ashamed of her lack of knowledge. Both the rape and the aftermath exposed her vulnerabilities, and she was humiliated.

After the police have investigated a crime scene, collected evidence, and taken testimonies, the yellow tape comes down and business returns to normal. Not so for a survivor of acquaintance rape. When a woman is raped, her body is desecrated; the temple has been violated. Healing of her sacred body is directly connected to healing of her soul. When the victim is Christian, she is a member of the body of Christ and a creation embodied by God; violence to a woman's body affects her faith and her ability to make meaning. The physical damage done to an acquaintance rape survivor is most immediately obvious in the desecration of her body. Cuts, bruises, flashbacks, long-term infections, muscle soreness, and more serve as signs of the violence. But these outward and visible signs point to an inward and spiritual terror caused by the rape.[17]

Survivors of all sorts of crimes have a strong reaction to the location of the crime. Wanting to get far away from the location is a natural response. When the scene of the crime is the body itself, running is not only difficult but can take on very destructive behaviors for survivors. Eating disorders, sexual promiscuity, suicidal ideations and attempts, alcohol abuse, and self-cutting can be attempts to run from the scene. In the end, they merely add to the desecration.

Humiliation and Notions of Purity

Humiliation is a common feeling for survivors. Their way of being in the world has been assaulted, and they feel degraded. After the rape, survivors are highly vulnerable because their sense of self has been shattered. Interacting in the world with a desecrated understanding of one's own being is frightening and devastating. On college campuses, this devastation takes the form of the "walk of shame."[18] The morning after a party, when a woman is leaving the fraternity house where she had too much to drink and was unable to avoid unwanted sexual activity, she steps into the world recognizing that no one will believe that she was raped. She even doubts herself. Head down and feeling isolated, she takes a step out the door and begins her walk of shame.

Rape by an acquaintance is particularly humiliating when the woman has never experienced consensual sexual intimacy. When Debra was raped, she was sexually inexperienced. The flow of blood after her rape signaled to her that her virginity had been "stolen." She was devastated. She understood her virginity as a gift to be saved for a future husband, and now she was "damaged goods." Thirty years after her rape, Debra still mourns the loss of her virginity.

Throughout Christian history, virginity has been equated with a woman's spiritual valor. It has been thought to determine a woman's purity and devotion. "For the religious woman a preserved hymen may not guarantee entrance into heaven but the inappropriate loss of the hymen diminishes the chances for eternal salvation."[19] While physically the hymen (the symbol of virginity) may be ruptured during rape, so too can it be ruptured by a tampon or in a biking accident. Rape is no more related to a person's first sexual experience than is a woman's first gynecological examination.[20]

The importance of virginity became all too clear to me one evening when, while staffing the rape-crisis hotline, I received a call from the hospital requesting support. Arriving at the emergency room, I was directed to a small room, where I found two police officers, a specially trained nurse, and Loreena,[21] a twelve-year-old Latina. She had been digitally penetrated (and perhaps more) by a young man. After the police finished getting the information, the nurse, Loreena, and I went to the examination room where she was instructed to strip down and lie on the table. While the nurse gently probed, photographed, and looked for any evidence of the violence, I stood beside Loreena, explaining the procedure and holding her hand. When the nurse stepped out to talk to the police, Loreena asked me, "Am I still a virgin?" To this young Latina, virginity was important. She knew, as well, that it was important to her father. I assured her that she was still a virgin. "Even if this man put his penis in you, you did not agreed to it, and therefore it didn't 'count.'" Loreena was afraid that her stolen purity might ruin any future relationship with her family and with a future boyfriend or husband.

Virginity is a concept that is housed in a wider cultural context. In Latin communities, a combination of Roman Catholicism and machismo culture creates an environment in which women are to be protected by male family members.[22] A woman's sexual identity is closely tied to her family's place in the community. Virginity in this context takes on a communal dimension.

In her work on womanist suffering and resources of resistance, M. Shawn Copeland asserts that the lives, deaths, and survivings of enslaved black women force us to redefine idealized notions of long-suffering patience, love, hope, and faith. In slavery, the enormity of violence done to women decimated the virtuous notions of motherhood, virginity, and forgiveness. In their survivings, the survival skills of "motherwit," courage, physical resistance, and sass took on life-giving qualities that far outweighed the traditional Christian virtues. Regular degradation of black women forced them to claim these forms of resistance as new sources of life. "Because of the rape, seduction, and concubinage of Black women under chattel slavery, chastity or virginity begs new meaning."[23] The very existence of such violence demands that we find new redemptive definitions of chastity or virginity. When a woman is raped, virginity must be given new meaning. Its place as a virtue must be redefined. If women are to claim new meanings of virginity, they must first name the role it plays in the larger community's identity. Only then can a survivor begin to reconfigure the role it plays in her own trauma, desecration, and healing.

Healing after the violence of acquaintance rape means reclaiming the desecrated body and healing the scene of the crime. It requires a cleansing of the woman's body and a cleansing of her devastated self-concept. After a rape, survivors want to shower away the violence. Melanie even used this language of cleansing showers as she reflected on the power of prayer. Survivors report standing in the shower for hours trying to wash away the terror and reclaim the ownership of their bodies. A woman's feeling of desecration and contamination can be that much harder when, after the rape, she is instructed not to shower if evidence is to be collected. Violence to a survivor's body profoundly affects her understanding of how she lives in the world. In the act of rape, a body is deemed unimportant and unworthy. Healing from rape entails reclaiming the sacredness of the body, even in its brokenness.

The Loss of "Normal" and a Rape Schedule

Women who have been raped split their lives into pre-rape and post-rape time. Pre-rape, women were safe and things made sense, friends were trustworthy, and evil was mostly "out there." A post-rape existence ushers in a mourning for the lost past, suffering in the present, and a fear that the survivor will always feel this way. Living between mourning and lost dreams can feel like being sentenced to hell. Survivors mourn the loss of pre-rape life; they mourn the loss of "normal." All of the women in this study mourned this loss of a familiar way of being. Hannah forgot her ATM card access number and her own phone number. She couldn't call home without looking up her mom's phone number. She kept bumping into a loss of everyday knowledge. Losing the small details of everyday knowledge is disorienting. Debra's loss of normalcy came as she chose to protect her community from any knowledge of her rapes. Her once-safe community became vulnerable to her own powerful secret. Protecting the community's "normal" took precedence over her own needs. In time, Debra's "normal" became a raging storm of anger. Melanie tried to hold onto her former world by avoiding a name for the rape. Abby felt alone in her otherness and missed her own familiarity. This newness was not welcome.

Ruth Krall equates this loss of normalcy with the loss of an "assumptive world."[24] A woman's assumptive world involves a belief in her own invulnerability in a world that has order and allows her some control. Rape and its aftermath shatter this world. When these assumptions crumble, a woman experiences shock, confusion, helplessness, and terror. In turn, she can lose her guiding system; she loses her ability to understand human relational behavior. This is especially true when a woman is raped by an acquaintance.

Before rape, much of a survivor's worldview is intuitive and unconscious; she can easily believe that she is invulnerable to rape if she is careful about what she does, where she goes, and with whom she spends time. When rape occurs, this assumptive, intuitive world is shattered. After the rape, she must create a new set of expectations about life. When every action and reaction feels new and conscious, a survivor's life becomes one of intention. Constant and deliberate intentionality is draining. After being raped, sheer survival pushes a woman to reexamine her values. This she must do over and over, and this is exhausting.

Judith Herman discusses this lost assumptive environment in terms of a nonfunctioning system of self-protection. Traumatic reactions, she suggests, occur when the system is faced with no viable choice. When neither resistance nor escape is possible, the human system of self-defense becomes overwhelmed and disorganized. A traumatized person can feel and act as though her nervous system has been disconnected from the present.

Each component of the ordinary response to danger, having lost its effectiveness, tends to continue in an altered and exaggerated state long after the actual danger is over. Trauma tears apart a complex system of self-protection that normally functions in an integrated way. "Traumatic events destroy the victim's fundamental assumptions about the safety of the world, the positive value of the self, and the meaningful order of creation."[25]

When rape shatters a person's system of self-protection, her inner guiding rules change. Rape contradicts the ordinary rules of living. "She/he has experienced the something that she/he thinks only happens to other people, the something that contradicts the ordinary 'rules' of one's environment. The world is no longer a hospitable place. A rape victim's life will never be the same again."[26] She has been here before, but nothing looks the same. It is a mind game. She no longer knows *how* she knows *what* she knows. It is a shattering of her ability to "make sense." Rape provokes a crisis of knowledge and a crisis in the act of knowing itself.

Acquaintance rape forces a woman to question *how* she knows. At the same time, it forces her to struggle with *who* she is as she tries to relate to others. Rape by an acquaintance goes to the core of a woman's self-identity in that it calls into question how she can be in community. Distress following rape stems not only from the violent act itself, but from the resulting feeling that formerly trusted people are no longer trustworthy. If a woman no longer knows whom to trust (given that the person who violated her was an acquaintance), can she even trust herself? For Monique Savage, Director of the Goldsmith Counseling Center at Adrian College in Michigan, the struggle she sees in college women is clear. When a young woman is raped by an acquaintance, her familiar life and world suddenly become foreign. Into this foreign world survivors are not eager to venture. "On a practical level the survivor can say she is feeling badly and she is scared to come out because the perpetrator is still around. On a deeper level it's 'I don't even know who I am; I don't know how to present myself in the world anymore.'"[27] The fear is not only that the survivor can be re-violated, but that she is now in a world with no sense of who she is in it. A woman's knowing who she is and how she knows it is a fundamental skill of living in community.

Mourning the loss of a violence-free, pre-rape life suggests that violence is not normative. Unfortunately, for many women this is only an illusion. With statistics suggesting that one in four girls is sexually assaulted before age eighteen, a large percentage of women do not have the privilege of assuming safety.[28]

Living with the knowledge that rape can happen means women live with an ever-shrinking present reality. When the sun is up, women live in the public, in the open. They can go about their business with relative safety (and this is only relative; acquaintance rape calls this into question). But, once the sun goes down, women's freedom is limited. Women have a shorter day to be publicly productive. For many women, going to the grocery store at night means asking, "Do I need this item so much that I am willing to endure the anxieties of being out?" Filling the gas tank at night or going to the ATM after dusk becomes a rape-defying task. Nighttime means every public decision is a choice between need and risk. Living on a rape schedule, women have a shrinking day. Survivors are more aware of this than anyone.

As children, many girls unknowingly learn this rape schedule from their mothers. Safe neighborhood hangouts become off limits when the sun goes down. On a college campus, women know the rape schedule. All around the campus, nighttime escort services are advertised for women students and faculty. Take Back the Night marches become yearly events. Nighttime on a college campus means being in groups, being escorted, or staying inside. Going outside at night requires prior planning. Spontaneity becomes a risky business; it can even be seen as suggesting a woman's willingness to be assaulted. The irony, of course, is that women are more at risk once they get *in* their residence halls and homes than when they are traveling to them. Whether it is living on a rape schedule or mourning the loss of a once-safe world, acquaintance rape can have a devastating effect on the survivor's experience of living in community.

Trauma to Communal Ties

The trauma experienced in the body of the woman can be matched by the trauma she undergoes in the larger body of the community. This creates in her a fundamental disturbance. Abby did not know other women who had been raped and was now having to create her own path of healing. With no role models or friends to follow, she felt isolated. She did not have a language to describe her feelings and could not find community around the experience. Abby was raped at an age when the task of the young adult woman is to explore her identity. For a woman, this identity journey is intimately entwined with her connection to her peers and the wider community. When Abby's connection to her friends and community changed, it directly affected her identity. She became Other. What was once home became separate and unknown. When this happened, Abby felt alienated.

Secrets can also have negative effects on one's sense of community. Debra did not tell anyone about her rapes for many years. She felt that there was too much to risk; Debra was concerned that the knowledge of the rapes would devastate her world. Keeping the secret was thus her way of protecting her family and the community. Further, as an African American, her world was vulnerable to the wider racist community. Telling her secret would have put her world at even more risk of violence. She could not risk making her community vulnerable by telling her secret so, for the sake of her community, Debra chose to tell no one. Debra's decision to protect her community meant sacrificing her own place in it.

Being in community means having intimate relationships. Acquaintance rape changes how a woman develops future relationships. As eschatological people, Christians live with the realized hope that the future holds promise and new life. These hopes and dreams serve as sources of newness and grace. Acquaintance rape can interfere with these hopes. Both Debra and Hannah noted that they use their rape stories to assess men. They both have used their rape stories as a litmus test to see if the men could bear their pain. If the men could hear their stories and understand the implications of the suffering, they could be trusted. At the time of this research, no men had passed the test. When trust is betrayed by an acquaintance, the rape itself can become a gauge of the trustworthiness of members of the community.

Healing a Shattered World

Acquaintance rape survivors experience psychospiritual shattering in the form of betrayal, problems in naming, self-blame, desecration of the body, loss of normalcy, and devastation to one's place in the community. But the story does not end there. Evil does not win. Acquaintance rape is not a terminal diagnosis nor a permanent banishment to hell. Healing of the psychospiritual trauma involves meaning-making, acting to redeem the violence, salvific anger, and reclaiming the healing power of the community.

Meaning-Making as Healing
Making or finding meaning becomes a source of healing for the survivor in the aftermath of rape and contributes to the reconstruction of her world. Acquaintance rape shatters the woman's process of knowing and severs her ties to a community that gives meaning to her being. When this meaning-making environment is devastated, its reconstruction takes both time and the ability to integrate the knowledge of the violence back into the newly constructed psychospiritual environment. This meaning-making activity is a natural response to the trauma, yet

it pushes survivors to do very difficult work. Herman sees it as a reconstruction of the trauma story:

> Reconstructing the trauma story . . . includes a systematic review of the meaning of the event, both to the patient and to the important people in her life. The traumatic event challenges an ordinary person to become a theologian, a philosopher, and a jurist. The survivor is called upon to articulate the values and beliefs that she once held and that the trauma destroyed. She stands mute before the emptiness of evil, feeling the insufficiency of any known system of explanation. Survivors of atrocity of every age and every culture come to a point in their testimony where all questions are reduced to one, spoken more in bewilderment than in outrage: Why? The answer is beyond human understanding.[29]

Making sense out of nonsensical violence can feel self-defeating. Kathleen Sands contends that the only reason violence does not make sense is that we cannot allow such chaos to be normal. When we are not able to find meaning in and out of the chaos of violence, we make evil untouchable.[30] It feels dangerous to try to make meaning out of violence, pain, and suffering because it feels like any such attempt either directly or tacitly justifies the evil, pain, and suffering. To make meaning after rape, we must be clear that survivors are not looking for meaning *in* evil and violence, but meaning *out of* violence, that is, in the healing. In so doing, survivors avoid anything that approaches a justification of evil.

Trying to find meaning in the aftermath of acquaintance rape is a common response of survivors. Marie Fortune suggests that this is the primary motivation behind the "if only I hadn't done . . ." thought process.[31] The why question is both a practical and philosophical move. It is an attempt to understand the cause and effect of the rape, but it can also be an attempt to regain some control over the situation. After the rape, a woman will focus on details as a way to try to regain some control. If she can figure out why the rape happened, she might reason, she can prevent it from happening again. Fortune asserts, "On the whole, this effort to understand the 'why' of one's victimization is a healthy sign. It is in fact an effort to regain some semblance of control of one's life and environment, i.e., to regain that which was lost in the assault."[32]

The women in this study used embodied and active images to describe the meaning-making process. Hannah understood it as enduring the worst and learning that she could survive it. Debra used the active metaphors of "letting go of the storm," "filling up the empty," and "finishing the work of Dinah and Tamar." These metaphors suggest that healing involves the hard work of weathering the suffering, replenishing the soul, and recognizing communal connections. An essential component of healing from acquaintance rape is being and feeling believed. Throughout her court proceedings, Hannah had a supportive network that believed her. They believed that she was good, that she had been raped, that she did not deserve it, and that she needed restitution. Being believed was empowering. It enabled her to claim her own voice.

The healing that comes from finding or making meaning is not a one-time event or a core disposition; it is a process. To heal from acquaintance rape is to be on a journey marked by insights and small successes. Melanie has not found a name for her violation. To continue to move beyond the power of the rape, she will need to name it. When she does, it will be both a relief and a struggle. Rebuilding trust, listening to intuitions, and learning to operate in a different world are not instantaneous skills. Rape is a crime of the soul, and healing the soul takes time.

In this research, I was surprised by the number of ways the survivors attempted to make sense of the rapes. One survivor seemed to belittle both the rape and her response to it: It was "no big deal" and "she didn't really care." These responses seemed so incongruous with the other parts of her story that I assumed it was denial or minimization. Upon reflection, I wonder if these were her attempts to make sense of the situation, a bit at a time. Rather than minimizing the event or her suffering, she was trying to place it in a larger context so that the evil would not overwhelm her. For several survivors, coping took the form of the suspension of their own interpretations of the situation—they asked their friends and family if they defined the event as rape. Two of the survivors even asked the rapist. Suspending one's own terrible interpretation in search of a better interpretation is part of the meaning-making process. What is seen as denial and minimization can easily be interpreted as a problematic coping mechanism. But for survivors, it may be one mechanism in a long-term process of healing.

The process of making sense as a function of healing requires chronological distance from the rape. It is not something that can happen when the woman is in a survival mode. It requires the ability to be introspective and the ability to transcend the experience. To do so, the survivor must first name and then begin to deal with the psychospiritual trauma of betrayal. Debra and Melanie taught me much about this process. Debra had the most distance from her rape and had more time to find meaning in the event. Her interview was filled with metaphorical language and transcendent comments. She spoke of her healing as the completion of the work of Dinah and Tamar, anger as a stalker, and grieving as freedom. Debra was able to step back enough from her trauma to reflect on it. Melanie, on the other hand, was not able to do this. Because she was struggling to name the violence and figure out her culpability in it, she was not able to be metaphorical about the experience. Melanie had a difficult time reflecting on her healing process or making sense of the experience. For her, the interview was difficult. I was unknowingly pushing her to find sense where there was none. Imposing meaning on a survivor's experience is not healing.

Refusing Evil the Last Word

Meaning-making involves cognitive and psychospiritual work. It also involves refusing to let evil have the last word. Healing involves "giving back" and "making a difference." The four women offered to participate in this study because they each believed it would help other acquaintance rape survivors and religious professionals. In helping others, they knew they were helping themselves. Hannah called it "cleaning up her karma." For all the women, giving back by participating in this study was proof that evil did not have the last word. "A light shines in the darkness and the darkness does not overcome it" (John 1:5). Acquaintance rape changes the course of a woman's life, but it does not completely defeat her. A violence defined by a taking away is redeemed by a giving back.

Anger Is Salvific When It Is Not a Way of Life

Righteous anger, that is, anger at an injustice, is salvific and a crucial step for survivors of acquaintance rape. It plays an important part in the healing of a survivor's psychospiritual world. When betrayal and lack of trust leave a survivor feeling confused and lost, anger can help her regain her footing and claim that she was not at fault. Hannah had a hard time functioning after the rape. She was suicidal and had a difficulty remembering details. She decided to press charges, but she felt confused and lonely. Hannah's epiphany came when an unacceptable plea bargain was offered. She considered it, until a friend suggested this was all she could really expect. In that moment, Hannah felt complete rage. Accepting the plea bargain felt like acceptance of the rape. Hannah's rage motivated her to continue with the court case and testify. Marie Fortune asserts that righteous anger, originating in God's commitment to each person's wholeness, is the body and soul's response to the embodiment of evil. It is the refusal to let evil be normative.[33] Hannah's anger was an investment in this larger hope; Hannah's anger was salvific.

Though anger can be salvific, for many women it is not an easy thing to experience. Many women have been socialized by their faith traditions and other aspects of culture to repress or deny their anger. Because the expression of anger for some women is counter-cultural, expressing it can be frightening. Anger, however, is an important part of the healing process. Acquaintance rape survivors rarely feel anger immediately following rape. Anger is not an immediate survival response; betrayal, confusion, and fear are. For a survivor, anger is an indication that she has made it far enough along in her healing to have a sense of her power. Anger requires power. Acquaintance rape can strip a survivor of her confidence. Anger can be an important source of reclaiming her right to Be. Focused anger is a declaration that surely she is made in the image of the Great I Am.

Hope for healing is itself grounded in a partnership of righteous anger and a commitment to truth.[34] Revenge, as distinguished from righteous anger, can cut off the possibility for justice and can become self-destructive. As Jesus demonstrated with the moneychangers, righteous anger can move us to stop the violation of the temple (the body). Anger is a stage in the healing process and not a way of life; when directed properly, it can be healing.

Friends and family can experience an overwhelming wash of anger after a rape. This can become problematic when their anger overshadows the survivor's response. Rage and desire for retaliation are commonly experienced by supportive family, friends, and religious professionals. For a survivor, this rage is often not helpful. It can force a vulnerable survivor into feeling responsible for the support person's rage or even feeling the need to protect the rapist. He was an acquaintance (and possibly a friend) before he was a rapist. Abby felt overwhelmed by her parent's desire to attack her rapist. Their rage got in the way of her healing. When supportive persons express rage to the survivor, they become unavailable as a healing community.

Anger is an important part of the healing when it helps the survivor take charge of her healing. When anger becomes a way of life, however, it can be destructive. Anger at the rapist and the rape is healthy and important because it redirects self-blame to the appropriate source. Detached from the event, however, anger can leave a survivor feeling powerless and trapped. Debra used three images to describe the powerful presence of her anger: peripheral vision, stalker, and ever-present clouds. As peripheral vision, anger gives a depth and dimension to any interaction and relationship. It literally gives shape to one's ability to operate in the world. As a stalker, anger is a lurking danger that compels a person to take precautions and change behaviors. And, as ever-present clouds, anger creates shadows and blocks the light. For Debra, anger was a dangerous, lurking, and defining experience that was keeping her on-guard. She needed release from the bondage of this anger.

Debra's release from thirty years of anger came when she made the decision to work on forgiveness. This forgiveness was not an exoneration of the rapist's behavior, a forgetting of the trauma, or a misappropriation of the blame, but a way to let the past be the past and move on, mourning all the losses and looking toward the hopes in the future. Debra desired a sense of reconciliation, not with the man who raped her, but with her own damaged relationship with God and herself. Forgiveness was the redemptive action that worked for Debra because she was in charge of it; she wanted to be released from the pervasive threat of her anger, and she needed to move on. As John Patton and Marie Fortune have suggested, forgiveness can only be life-giving when it is a byproduct of the total healing process.[35] Forgiveness is not redemptive when it is suggested as a way to bypass the suffering or to release the rapist from culpability. Nor does forgiveness work as a rite of exorcism by removing the pain, grief, and confusion. Forgiveness itself should never be an expectation of healing, and any suggestion of it by religious professionals should occur in the context of a wider notion of healing. To be authentic, forgiveness must start with the survivor naming the healing value of her righteous anger and then moving to self-compassion and a desire for right relations with the community and God. Forgiveness can be genuinely redemptive when it originates with and primarily benefits the survivor. Debra's pastor introduced the idea of forgiveness to her thirty years after the rape, and Debra considered it a welcome note of healing. She was consumed by her anger. In the end, forgiveness for her was not automatic or easy. But it was a release from anger as a way of life.

The Redemptive Power of Community

Healing a shattered world requires attention to communal relations. Rape by an acquaintance means that the violence springs from within a woman's communal network. Healing for a survivor means resanctifying a woman's redemptive community so that consent is understood and trust is reestablished. Mary Pellauer suggests:

> The woman victimized by rape, then, faces the interrelated tasks of healing her person and reconstituting her world. She must be healed, physically and emotionally. . . . At the same time, she must put her shattered world back together once again; she must learn situations that make her feel safe and secure once again. . . . She must come to terms with the naked face of terror once concealed in nebulous shadows.[36]

A supportive community becomes a crucial element in a survivor's attempt to reconstruct her psychospiritual world. Because the violence against her was done in her community, healing must occur there.

The community plays an integral role in providing a holding environment in which healing can happen. It includes helping the survivor name the violence and affirming that it was not her fault. Abby endured the terrible days after the rape because she had loving friends who believed her and did not minimize the violence, helped her name the violence, and did not abandon her in her suffering. Studies assert that survivors who have informal support networks to help them in their recovery will likely not experience PTSD and may not need professional mental-heath assistance. When this holding community is not present or is not considered a source of support, the survivor is left to struggle with betrayal and confusion on her own. The alienation experienced in the rape itself is exacerbated by the loneliness and the fear experienced in the silence. Religious professionals and faith communities have not generally been safe harbors for survivors because of their lack of knowledge and their confusion over sexual activity versus sexual violence. To be redemptive sources of support for survivors of acquaintance rape, religious professionals and faith communities must break their complicity with the silence, know the realities of the violence, and help create a space where survivors can find healing.

Acquaintance rape shatters a woman's psychospiritual world, devastating her ability to make sense of her environment, which, in turn, interferes with her ability to heal. This breakdown is neither a symptom of pathological dysfunction nor a sign that someone is predisposed to suffering. The betrayal, self-blame, and loss that occur can be healed through a long process of naming, claiming the power of the community, getting angry, and refusing to let evil have the final say.

The Good Samaritan Takes on the Virgin Mary

Earlier in this chapter, I introduced the notion of the Virgin Mary survivor as the archetype of the mythical "real rape" survivor. Returning to that notion, I believe there is a way to correct this harmful myth. Fortune uses the parable of the Good Samaritan as a metaphor for understanding and responding to sexualized violence. This parable highlights a central problem in understanding acquaintance rape. The parable of the Good Samaritan presents a story that is clear about the identity of the victim, the perpetrators, and the crime (Luke 10:29-37). It tells us the wrong response to the victim (passing by) and the right response (stopping, taking him to safety, giving resources, and checking back). It is all so clear. With acquaintance rape, we are not clear about the nature of the violence: Was it really rape or simply a bad evening? Nor are we clear about the identity of the true victim: Women who press charges are often told that they will ruin the man's reputation. When this happens, we do not know how or to whom to respond with compassion. A woman's trust is betrayed when she is raped by an acquaintance, leaving her confused and feeling alone. She blames herself, and so do others. "Real rape" myths confuse us. Because we do not understand the violence, we do not understand the identity of the victim. Survivors of acquaintance rape not only are blamed for their own complicity in the violence, but are also accused of being the violators themselves by falsely accusing men of rape. Using the parable of the Good Samaritan as a hermeneutical tool with acquaintance rape is valuable because it takes on the myth of the Virgin Mary survivor. We can only respond to the survivor on the side of the road when we understand the true nature of the violence and why we are so eager to pass on by.

An Additional Question for the Neighborly Samaritan

The self-defense training I was required to do as an advocate for a rape-crisis center was informative. I expected to learn ways to hit, punch, and gouge my way to a safer world. I learned some of that. More importantly, I learned that when a stranger comes to me and I feel threatened, I am to use my powerful voice to say no and get away from the situation. I need not tell him my name, give him directions, or help him find his dog. Because assailants often rely on a woman's willingness to suspend judgment, these self-defense lessons were training me to trust my intuition about situations and to respond in turn. Throughout the training, I was fascinated that I was having to learn that I owe nothing to a stranger in need. Or do I? The "do unto others" maxim of the Good Samaritan parable and the Golden Rule was telling me something different. Since childhood I have known the lesson about the Good Samaritan. That no-good duo who passed the beaten man and refused to give him the time of day deserved name-calling and finger-shaking. They did not stop. But the Samaritan, the stranger in their midst, stopped and helped. That is the gospel message. When I was not sure what else the tradition held, I was sure about helping my neighbor (even when I was not sure who my neighbor was.) For women who are reared with the gospel message of helping their neighbor, ingesting the self-defense notion of owing nothing to a stranger makes no sense. To make the parable of the Good Samaritan safe for women, we need to interpret it so that (1) we know *who* the victim is, (2) we do not have to sacrifice our safety to do it, and (3) we proclaim that sometimes saying no is the most life-giving message.

5

Pastoral Counseling and Acquaintance Rape

Religious professionals need help in working with survivors and their loved ones. This clergy person was no different:

> Kristen, I received a phone call from a young man whom I've never met. He called because he did not know whom else to call. His girlfriend, a member of my congregation, just told him that last year at school she was raped. I've talked to them, briefly, and they are struggling. The woman is uncharacteristically explosive, her parents aren't coping well, and the boyfriend just wants to be helpful. Kristen, if they come to my office for help, I'll be overwhelmed. What should I do?

General Guidelines

The goal of pastoral care and counseling with survivors of acquaintance rape is to listen, believe, provide information, be an advocate, and assist them in finding supportive sources of healing. This is the basis of an empowerment model of care. Debra named the counseling process as a holding onto hope until the survivor could find the hope herself. To empower women, religious professionals should attend to the following:

- Listen more than you talk. Whether you are the first person to hear the details or you are in a long line of supportive people, listen with an openness to a survivor's feelings, confusions, and pain. After assessing a woman's safety, keep questions about details to a minimum. Listening for details is important, but not at the expense of the feelings and cognitive confusions. In Debra's words, "Be willing to go to the tough places."

- Name the violence. Be attentive to the words that a survivor uses, but do not introduce euphemisms for the violence. Name it acquaintance rape. Without this primary step, healing cannot happen. Melanie was unable to give a name to the violence and, as such, was struggling.
- Affirm that it was not her fault. This will need to be repeated over and over again because a survivor's self-blame, confusion, and sense of betrayal, coupled with social messages of blame, will have her believing otherwise. Naming it acquaintance rape and affirming that she was not at fault were foundational for Abby's healing. A year after the rape, she still needs to hear from many people that she was not at fault.
- Believe what a survivor tells you. It may sound too incredible, too painful, too dramatic, or just more than you can comprehend, but believe her. Suspend your own disbelief. Too many others will not. By believing her, you become a safe harbor. Be aware that even if you have examined your own beliefs about acquaintance rape distortions, it can be natural to try to distance yourself from the pain. A part of believing a survivor is not minimizing what she is saying or feeling. Acquaintance rape is not incidental, accidental, or bad sex. It is violence.
- Do not judge a survivor or her behaviors before, during, or after the rape. Only she knows what she was experiencing at the moment. Recognize that her choices in life may not be your choices. If you judge her or her behaviors, you cannot provide a safe enough space for her healing. If she feels judged, she will probably not come back to you for help.
- Validate her courage for coming to tell and assure her that you will keep this information confidential.
- Be a non-anxious presence that reacts to the reality of the rape. That is, empathically respond without letting the enormity of your feelings overwhelm her.

- A survivor can wonder if she is going crazy. Affirm that her feelings are a normal response to a very traumatic situation.
- Assess the availability of a healthy support system.
- Empower her to make her own decisions. Do not make them for her.
- If she has never spoken to a rape-crisis counselor or someone trained in matters of sexualized violence, explore this possibility.
- Use biblical and theological references and resources only as they are introduced by the survivor or when you are sure she welcomes them.
- Offer her readings that recount stories by other survivors and explain the distortions about rape.
- Limit self-disclosure of your own traumas.

Crisis Care

Religious professionals are most likely to learn a woman has been raped well after the rape. It is, however, important to know how to respond to a survivor at the time of the rape. If a woman comes to you within forty-eight hours of a rape:

- Assess her physical safety. Is she in immediate danger of further harm?
- Recommend that she wait to shower until after a medical examination.
- Suggest medical attention. Offer to go with her to the emergency room. If there is not a trained rape-support advocate, female clergy can offer to go into the exam room with her. Except in rare circumstances, male clergy should not.
- Explore with the victim the option of reporting the rape to the police. Respect her decision. Explain that she may choose to have the police collect evidence of the rape without pressing charges.

Additional Considerations

Beyond these, there are several matters for pastoral caregivers to understand when providing care to a survivor.

Affirming Survivors' Intuitive Skills

Recognizing a survivor's intuitive skills is key to empowering her. Intuition serves as a sensing device or a survival tool for interacting with the world. Marginalized peoples, in particular, have had to develop these well-honed intuitive skills to survive psychospiritually and physically. Religious professionals need to respect, rather than question, these skills. After a woman has been raped, feelings of uneasiness and hyperalertness are common. Changing telephone numbers, jobs, personal appearance, and communal habits can be common for survivors. Hannah moved across the country, and Debra could not tell anyone about her rapes until she had left her community. What may seem like unnecessary paranoia to even the most supportive care provider may feel imperative to a survivor. Only she knows her situation. Only she knows what will help her feel safe. It is important to encourage each survivor to listen to her intuitive or inner voice, even if her voice "sounds crazy." Many survivors question the "silliness" of their own inner voices. In one case, a woman said that she was too afraid to fall asleep at night. When asked what might help her feel safe enough, she answered, "having people sleep in the room with me." She was embarrassed because she said it felt so childish. After exploring this idea, she decided to ask two friends to join her in a "slumber party." In the aftermath of an acquaintance rape, a woman can severely doubt or belittle her own intuitive skills. Helping a survivor reclaim respect for her intuitive skills can be an important task for pastoral care providers. This can involve helping her to see that her "inner voice" is actually a well-developed tool stemming from her synthesis of many environmental clues.

Recognizing the Role of the Survivor's Anger

A survivor of acquaintance rape rarely experiences anger immediately following the rape (acute phase), when she is in survival mode. Anger is not typically part of that process. When it does emerge, it can be a sign that healing is taking place. Anger signals the survivor's reclaiming of her voice and her power. Anger was crucial in Hannah's healing process. It was when she became angry at the defense attorney's proposed plea bargain that she was finally able to reclaim some of her power. She stopped feeling tremendous fear and started feeling rage and indignation. Working with and not against anger is crucial. Many women struggle with the appropriateness of anger, and yet the faith community has not been a helpful resource for this struggle. Religious professionals should be aware that, to the survivor, they could represent the source of guilt that accompanies their anger. Religious professionals can help women claim the life-giving nature of their anger and help them express it in ways that do not endanger the survivor or her place in her community.

Anger as a response to the rape and the rapist is part of the healing process and is healthy. Separated from its source, however, anger can be problematic. It may take a long time for a survivor to feel anger toward her rapist. This was true for Debra. At the time of the rapes, Debra could not express any of her feelings related to them. Debra moved on from the rapes, but her feelings did not. As Debra aged, her anger was no longer connected to the rapes but became a way of life. Debra felt stalked by her anger. It consumed her. This disconnected anger became debilitating. When she reached that point, she had to do something. Her pastor suggested that it was time she forgive the rapist and move on. For Debra, thirty years after the rapes, this felt like a life-giving option.

In religious circles, talk about anger is often connected to issues of forgiveness. Nevertheless, forgiveness, as a religious resource, is a complex thing for religious professionals to suggest.

The suggestion made sense to Debra because it was a way to move beyond the disconnected anger. She wanted to feel something else, and the forgiveness introduced this possibility. When considering forgiveness as a religious resource to offer, religious professionals should understand forgiveness in the wider context of violence, power, and healing. Forgiveness should not be introduced if the survivor is feeling confused or threatened by her rapist. Nor is forgiveness a means to bypass healthy aspects of anger. And it should never be seen as a means to exorcise the painful feelings. Three of the women in the study could not have engaged in a conversation about forgiveness because either their anger was helping them make sense of the rape or, in Melanie's case, she was not yet able to feel angry.

Accessibility of a Religious Professional and the Faith Community

When a woman is raped, she has to make a decision about whom she will tell. For some, clergy are a known and trusted source of comfort and support. Religious professionals may have an advantage over mental heath professionals in that they may have a relationship with the survivor prior to the rape. In embattled communities, religious professionals may be the primary or only source of help available. My own introduction to acquaintance rape came when, as a college chaplain, I was sought out by women survivors for support. They knew that I would be open to listening because I facilitated residence-hall programs on sexualized violence. In most cases, the women who came to me had previous connections with home congregations and pastors who had been sources of support.

Even when religious professionals communicate their openness to talking about violence, many women facing the stigmatizing trauma of acquaintance rape may avoid religious professionals. They can fear disbelief, judgment, ostracism, and lack of support by them. This is especially true when the faith community, like the larger society, sees sexualized violence as an "unmentionable sin."[1] Perceptions of the religious official play a role in a victim's hesitancies in seeking them out for help. If the religious professional is perceived as lacking knowledge, sensitivity, and experience in working with assault, survivors may avoid them. Because the betrayal of trust is at the heart of acquaintance rape, levels of trust and competence assumed in other pastoral situations are not sufficient in working with these survivors. This is *not* the time for the clergyperson to learn on the job. Being open to working with a survivor is important, but it is not enough. A religious professional competent to work with survivors of acquaintance rape needs to communicate to the survivor that it is acceptable to talk about rape in the congregation, that she or he is knowledgeable, and that she or he has some experience in helping survivors. This can happen with the help of church newsletters, sermons, educational events, and bulletin boards. Both Debra and Melanie asserted that knowing about acquaintance rape is important, but when the religious professional does not have all the answers, they should be forthright about it. For Melanie, it is a matter of trust: If clergy and others are honest about the limits of their knowledge and experience with survivors, they are more trustworthy. Even when a religious professional feels equipped and trustworthy, a survivor may not share with them their story of rape and betrayal.

Professional Limitations and Referrals

An important part of working with survivors of acquaintance rape is knowing your professional limits. Clergy need to state when they are inexperienced or too under-trained to help. Having good pastoral care and counseling skills is not enough. Some degree of specialized knowledge is necessary to respond effectively. To work toward this competency, clergy need to develop a level of comfort in working with issues of sexualized violence. This means both being aware of their own strong feelings about the horror of rape and having the ability to talk comfortably about sex and anger. A high percentage of acquaintance rapes involve the use of alcohol and other drugs. For three of the four survivors, alcohol or drugs were involved in the rape event (two of the women were drunk and one perpetrator was high). Given this, religious professionals must also be able to talk about the use of alcohol and other drugs without being judgmental or moralistic.

When a survivor is in the acute phase, religious professionals should refer a victim to specialized agencies prepared to deal with sexualized violence. They know the legal and medical procedures and can help minimize the trauma of the process for survivors. For a survivor who is further along in her healing but who has not had adequate support from friends and family, a referral may also be necessary. Having a current list of referrals is crucial for religious professionals working with survivors. When making a referral, it is preferable to refer to someone that the religious professional knows and trusts. Wise use of referrals comes from self-awareness, knowing your own limitations, and being clear about your own role as a religious professional. Care should be taken so that the survivor does not feel as though she has been "dumped." Acquaintance rape is an issue for pastoral care, and a referral that comes too quickly can imply that a minister believes it falls outside her or his duties. Before religious professionals refer, they must be good listeners. Once a referral is made, it does not preclude the pastoral care provider from attending to the survivor's psychospiritual needs, such as helping her identify supportive individuals and communities and offering her the rich liturgical resources of the faith tradition.

Struggles of the Empathic Relationship

A religious professional's ability to be effectively present with a survivor of acquaintance rape rests on the demands of an empathic relationship. Being a non-anxious presence in the midst of pain and betrayal, and having the capacity to hear the stories without minimizing, pathologizing, or running from them, is a grueling task. A caregiver's ability to do this is a gift that helps a woman heal.

It can be difficult to maintain a non-anxious presence in the face of enormous anxiety, rage, and despair. Being present to survivors and encouraging their expression of feelings can mean care providers become the first to receive the survivor's accumulated rage and anguish. Recognizing this possibility can help the care provider avoid personalizing explosions and honor them without accepting blame for the trauma. This can also lay the groundwork for a deeply trusting relationship. Emma Justes asserts that if pastoral counselors are unable to work with women's anger, they should not be doing pastoral counseling with women.[2]

Working with a survivor of acquaintance rape can be draining. Because a survivor's experience can be raw and painful, pastors may feel overwhelmed by the survivor's extreme sadness, rage, and vulnerability. In the midst of this, religious professionals may be tempted to disavow their own feelings of anger and their own capacity for evil. They can feel threatened by the survivor's helplessness and their own inability to help. As such, they may succumb to the trap of rescuing or taking premature action on behalf of the survivor. This can lead to boundary violations and a fostering of unhealthy dependency on the part of the survivor. Religious professionals can also fall into the trap of trying to pull survivors along in their recovery. A caregiver's attempt to move someone along can be an indication that the survivor's story is causing the professional to feel anxious. It can be an attempt to alleviate his or her own anxieties. When this happens, the caregiver's feelings become the guiding force for the survivor's healing and recovery. Debra knows that talking about rape is difficult. She wanted clergy to know that their role is to be in the storm with the survivors, helping to create a space where survivors can express their strong feelings. This, she said, is the greatest gift a pastor can give: to be with the survivor and not ahead of her. Anxieties of caregivers are normal struggles inherent in working with survivors. Only in accepting them as natural (rather than seeing them as aberrations or weaknesses) can caregivers reflect on them and keep from acting on them.

One of the ways religious professionals try to push survivors along in their healing is through the misuse of religious resources. Quoting scriptures and offering prayers and words of hope can be important resources for religious professionals, but only if they are consistent with the expectations and needs of the survivors. This is not the time for evangelism. In fact, religious resources used inappropriately or at the wrong time can add to the survivor's shame and sense of betrayal. Three of the four women in this study named their concern about poorly timed religious offerings. Debra indicated that while a survivor is in the midst of suffering, words of comfort that say or imply "good can come out of this" are not helpful. Hannah echoed this sentiment. Talking about God or God's love, she asserted, could be quite invasive. When a survivor does not love herself, it is hard to hear that others, even God, can do it better than she does. When a woman is vulnerable, "God-talk" may merely be, in Hannah's words, "meeting a quota" for the clergyperson. In the same way, Melanie implied that the use of biblical references could compromise the religious professional's ability to be helpful; instead of being a present advocate, they become "an examiner of faith."

When trying to decide whether to use religious resources (including prayers, sacraments, and scriptural references), religious professionals should ask:

- Whose purpose do they serve? Are they consistent with the survivor's beliefs or practices, or is the religious professional using them because she or he believes it will be good for the survivor?
- Who introduced them into the relationship? Did the survivor ask for prayer or biblical guidance, or did the care provider introduce them because they themselves find comfort in them?
- Are the religious resources offered in such a way that the survivor may decline them without feeling more guilt or shame?

- Did the survivor seek out the religious professional (in their role as pastoral caregiver), or is the religious professional making a pastoral call (as in a hospital setting or because someone asked them to talk to the woman)?
- Are the resources life-giving, or do they present a message that could leave the survivor feeling weak or judged?

As in the case of any pastoral care relationship, religious resources can be a tool for healing only when the survivor understands them as welcoming, helpful, and healing.

Pastoral countertransference can occur when the religious professional experiences a sense of vicarious trauma. Hearing a story of violation, betrayal, and fear can leave the religious professional feeling outraged or angry with the perpetrator and society. (This is true whether or not she or he is a survivor.) Verbally retaliating against the perpetrator may feel satisfying to the caregiver, but it can put the survivor in a compromised situation, especially if the rapist was a friend or lover. Calling the perpetrator names can force the survivor into a position of defending him, even if she is not clear what happened. I have known the feeling of wanting to harm a rapist. My anger came through in my nighttime dreams and my daytime fantasies. When this happens, it is important to talk to a colleague, pastoral counselor, spiritual director, or therapist. Do not ask the survivor to deal with your vicarious anger and trauma. Religious professionals need to be aware that their need for justice or retribution may not be the survivor's need.

Male Religious Professionals

Support, reassurance, and trust are important issues for survivors of acquaintance rape. The gender of the careprovider may play a role in whether the survivor can work with them. For some, a male religious professional can be very reassuring. For Abby, the gender of her male counselor did not bother her. She felt heard and affirmed by him. At the same time, she was aware that male friends could not be empathic. For others such as Melanie, male caregivers could never provide her a safe enough pastoral relationship because they could never have an embodied knowledge of her experience. Only the survivor can determine this. Male religious professionals should be prepared for this reality and refer the survivor to a skilled female pastoral counselor when needed. In either case, it is important that the male religious professional is neither patronizing nor protective. A survivor does not need a rescuer but someone who will listen and support. Moreover, male pastoral caregivers should especially avoid any action that might be perceived by the survivor as physically or sexually threatening: touching should be kept to a minimum; and approaching a survivor from behind when she does not know a man is there can be threatening. Playfulness can easily be misconstrued and does not help a survivor trust even the most caring man.

Following Up with a Survivor
Rape trauma can affect a woman for months and years. Unlike individuals who have experienced traumas related to deaths or naturally occurring events ("acts of God"), an acquaintance rape survivor does not have a way to publicly grieve the suffering and permanent change brought on her by the rape. Survivors may need help in mourning losses that come from being raped. The failure to complete the normal process of grieving can in fact perpetuate the traumatic reaction. In ordinary bereavement, social rituals contain and support a mourner through the process. In the absence of such support, the potential for pathological grief and persistent depression is extremely high. There are no public or private rituals of mourning for survivors of acquaintance rape. This is the place where faith communities could fit naturally because of their fundamental commitments to theological paradigms that value the power of rituals. Helping survivors ritualize their mourning and their healing—for example, offering prayer services for all survivors of trauma or recognizing October as

Domestic Violence Awareness Month—could be a way for faith communities to honor survivors.

Confronting the Rapist

Survivors may want to confront their rapists. Three of the survivors in this study personally confronted the men who raped them. One used the legal system to do it. All of them were internally motivated to speak to the men and did not respond well when others suggested they should press charges. They confronted the men because they were seeking clarity ("Did this really happen?"), and they were claiming the right to name the violence ("You raped me; this is how it has affected me; and you caused it.") The two women who personally confronted the men did so because they continued to live in the same close-knit community with the men. They refused to feel like strangers in their own environments. None of the men admitted that what he had done was rape or voluntarily took responsibility for his action. One man was forced to do so by the courts.

Religious professionals should never introduce the idea of confronting the perpetrator. If the survivor wants to confront him, the religious professional should help her assess how safe she will be and feel and what she hopes to gain. There are some good reasons for a woman to confront her rapist: claiming her voice, naming the truth, taking back her power, demanding justice, and even warning the community. But getting him to voluntarily accept responsibility for his actions (as opposed to having the courts "help" him do this) or providing the survivor a suitable explanation for his actions is not likely to happen.

Emergency Rooms, Police, and the Courts

When a survivor confides in a religious professional, the caregiver should inform her of the benefits of notifying legal authorities. The police can serve as a part of the team that attends to the needs of the victim. The police can help by affirming the reality of the crime and getting her needed medical attention. If the police are called, the woman is not required to press charges later.

When a survivor goes to an emergency room, she will interact with medical personnel and law enforcement officers. Before a thorough medical exam, the police will take her statement. Many hospitals will welcome an advocate to be with the woman during this conversation. Because the police can ask very direct and descriptive questions, an advocate, whether someone from a crisis center or clergy, should be sensitive to how humiliating this can be for the survivor.

If a woman thinks she wants to press charges and the rape happened within forty-eight hours of reporting it, the hospital—on behalf of the legal system—will administer a rape kit. The cost of this is completely covered by the local police.

Once police officers have taken the victim's detailed statement, a medical professional (presumably specially trained) will check her body for physical trauma and evidence of the rape. The administration of the rape kit involves combing her pubic hairs in search of foreign pubic hairs or foreign clothing fragments; photographing any bruises, scratches, or cuts on her arms, torso, legs, face, or genitals; checking under her finger nails for blood or skin; using a black light to search for semen (semen glows under ultraviolet light); and administering a pelvic exam. Because evidence is collected from her body, a victim who elects to go through the rape kit should wait to shower until after the procedure is complete. This in itself can be a difficult matter. The victim's clothes will be examined for signs of semen and blood and kept for evidence. Some hospitals or rape crisis centers will provide extra clothing for the victim to wear home; those that do not will depend upon the victim's family or friends to bring clothes.

The rape kit procedure can take several hours and can add to a victim's feeling of violation. The victim should therefore be advised about the procedure in advance and receive appropriate support during (when possible) and after the exam. Following the medical examination and rape kit, a detective attached to the police department's sex crimes unit will complete the investigation and will turn the case over to the prosecutor's office, who will determine if there is sufficient evidence to prosecute the crime. Because few rape cases make it through the legal system, it is important to help the victim/survivor understand that the rape need not meet the legal system's definition of rape for her to consider it a rape.

Apart from the legal matters, the hospital is charged with attending to the woman's physical trauma. With their primary focus on the present health of the woman, medical professionals are also charged with attending to questions about pregnancy, sexually transmitted diseases, and the use of date rape drugs. Before the woman leaves the hospital, she will be given the option of the morning-after pill to prevent pregnancy. Only five percent of rapes result in pregnancy, and yet survivors struggle with pregnancy as a terrorizing possibility.[3] Religious professionals should be aware that questions of pregnancy and conception intervention could be a difficult issue for some women.

Along with the question of pregnancy, survivors should be tested for sexually transmitted diseases (STDs). STDs are estimated to occur in up to 30 percent of rape victims.[4] Gonorrhea, chlamydia, neisseria, trichomonal infections, and syphilis are the most commonly seen; hepatitis B and human immunodeficiency virus (HIV) are life-threatening. Although the fear of STDs, including HIV and AIDS, is a major concern for women who are sexually assaulted, less than 27 percent of those who seek medical intervention receive any information or testing for exposure to HIV, and 39 percent receive no information about or testing for other STDs.[5] The possibility of infection from life-threatening viruses adds an additional long-term psychospiritual component to a survivor's response.

Information is just beginning to appear about the use of the illegal date rape drugs Rohypnol (flunitrazepam)—alias "ruphies," "circles," "Mexican valium," "rib," "roaches," "roach-2,"

"R-2,"—and GHB (gamma hydroxybutyrate)—alias "easy lay." Appearing on college campuses and in bars, these drugs are being used to incapacitate women. These tasteless sedatives are slipped into drinks and can lead to lethargy, a hypnotic state, passing out (losing consciousness), and blacking out (losing awareness of a block of time).[6] These drugs can leave women with no memory of the events that have occurred and unable to prove that they have been violated. The effects of these illegal drugs on long-term memory and healing are not yet known.

Family and Friends

Not all survivors of acquaintance rape will experience PTSD-like symptoms. Although there is no magic potion to warding off severe trauma responses, family and friends play a key role in the survivor's ability to make some sense of the experience and move on without traumatic repercussions. The severity and longevity of the trauma depend largely on how the survivor responds to those around her. If she feels comfortable in sharing what happened with those around her and finds a sensitive and caring response, then the recovery process can more easily proceed. Family and friends are often the first people victims go to and can be in the best situation to help. The survivor needs assurance that those whom she trusts enough to tell them about the incident care about *her*, and not primarily about the rape. Family and friends should invite the victim to talk about the rape and support her doing so but also respect her desire *not* to talk about it. Some women will not tell their family and friends because they believe their stories will devastate them. Melanie withheld her story from her parents to protect them. She did not want to tell many friends because she was afraid they would treat her differently. Although the weight of the secret was oppressive, Debra would not tell her family and friends because she was afraid her whole world would fall apart.

Rape's devastation does not stop with the survivor. It can have a strong effect on the victim's family. Religious professionals can play an important role in assessing the existence and health of a supportive system of family and friends. This can serve two purposes: to determine if they can be available to the survivor and to ensure that family and friends are getting their needs met. Religious professionals can be helpful to family and friends as they experience their own trauma and recovery process. People close to the survivor may give mixed messages, even blaming the victim through their expression of anger and pain. These concerned persons may need support and validation for their own losses, such as loss of intimacy, loss of interdependency, or loss of perceived ability to protect their loved one. Religious professionals can help concerned friends and family process their own feelings and not project them onto the survivor. Although rapes are hard on the whole family, it is important to help families remember that the precipitating crisis belongs to the victim. Careproviders should challenge family reactions that impede the victim's recovery.

Abby struggled with her parents' response to her rape. She valued their loving words but felt panicked by their vehemence about retaliating against the man who raped her. In her parents' minds, he was a rapist and a criminal. In Abby's mind, he was a friend, and she had been raped. Abby felt that if her parents had been able to talk to someone like a minister, it would have helped them and, in turn, her.

The Community of Faith and the Wider Community

Communities of faith have a wealth of resources that can help a survivor in her recovery process. Special liturgies for survivors of violence can be a powerful instrument of healing in pastoral care and counseling. They can provide occasions that represent many important aspects of healing: restoration of wholeness, redemption of dates and places, and the bold acclamation that the survivor is not alone. It should be cautioned that special liturgies can have the unintended effect of removing issues of violence from the mainstream of the congregation and, in so doing, minimizing the reality of the violence. Liturgies can never be a replacement for the hard process of grieving, raging, and recovery. Neither should they glorify victimhood. Authentic healing attends not only to wounds but to the restorative power of justice and envisioned wholeness.

The wider community plays a significant role in providing important resources for religious professionals and survivors. Clergy rarely have the time or the training to do all that is necessary with a victim of rape. In the same way, community agencies do not have the pastoral expertise to work with psychospiritual issues. It is important for pastoral careproviders to work out reciprocal referrals and training with other community health-care providers. To do this, religious professionals need to know and use community resources. There are many creative ways to do this. One congregation provided regular meeting space for two rape-support groups. They claimed it as part of their mission to the community and advertised it in their church bulletin. In so doing, they claimed their church as a community willing to talk about rape. This partnership between the church and the rape crisis agency also helped the agency, since the church provided a safe and anonymous place for survivors to gather and grieve. One additional development grew out of this partnership: The survivors took the initiative to talk about the role of the church and their faith in their healing processes.

Referral Resources

Pastoral care and counseling with survivors of acquaintance rape always involves knowing professional limits. The majority of trained religious professionals are not prepared to be thoroughly adequate rape counselors. They need not expect that of themselves. There are many community agencies and offerings that are important referral sources for professionals working with survivors of acquaintance rape.

Community Agencies and Other Resources

Rape-crisis centers are the best places to start because they have updated lists of local and regional services available to survivors (both those who press charges and those who do not). They have the most recent state regulations as well as information on advocacy, financial assistance, and support groups in the area. Some agencies also provide training programs for people in the community and community educators who will come to your congregation or group meeting. If they do not run a hotline, they will know who does.

Domestic violence shelters can also supply much of this information. They have the added resource of emergency housing if the survivor needs to relocate immediately.

The front of the phone book can provide information on *emergency hotline services,* including teen hotline numbers. State governments have worked hard to make such services available. In Connecticut, for instance, there is a state-run emergency hotline number (211) that will patch you through to other services. For a national listing of hotlines available, contact RAINN (Rape, Abuse, and Incest National Network) at 1-800-656-HOPE or http://www.rainn.org/counseling.html.

Planned Parenthood can be an important source of information on STDs and pregnancy concerns. They can provide referrals to clinics that do confidential HIV testing.

It is important to have available a *list of therapists and mental heath professionals* who are knowledgeable about sexualized violence. Do not assume that because someone is licensed they can work with survivors of acquaintance rape.

Include on your list *other religious professionals in your community* who are knowledgeable about this field. It is particularly important to find referral names and agencies in faith communities outside your own (e.g., Catholic Social Services,

Jewish Family Services, Salvation Army, Samaritan Pastoral Counseling Centers).

The Center for the Prevention of Sexual and Domestic Violence is an important source of information for Christian, Jewish, and Muslim communities. Along with videos, literature, a newsletter, and speakers, they have an up-to-date listing of religious professionals across the country who are knowledgeable advocates for survivors and their families (http://www.cpsdv.org).

Legal Assistance

It is important to have information about legal options for survivors. As noted, rape-crisis centers often have this information. If such a center is not accessible, it is helpful to have information on the following:

Local police departments often have an on-call officer designated to work with sexualized violence, particularly with children. Police can be called for assistance whether or not the survivor chooses to press charges.

The *District Attorney's (DA's) office* can provide helpful information on procedures and regulations.

Victim witness or victim assistance programs are often housed in the DA's office and can provide a supportive advocate to be with a survivor if she decides to press charges or testify in court. These programs are funded through court costs from convicted perpetrators.

Temporary restraining orders (TROs) can be initiated through the local police and can be used when a survivor is feeling that the perpetrator is continuing to threaten her physically. Be aware that a TRO is only as effective as the person who abides by it and that it requires the survivor to go fill out paperwork and pay a fee. Talk with the survivor about where she will go and what she will do if the TRO escalates the situation.

Medical Assistance

Many emergency rooms are equipped to help women who have been raped. They will often have a separate space so that victims do not have to sit in the public waiting room. Some hospitals have SARTs—sexual assault response teams. A SART nurse or physician can be a godsend at such a time because she or he is likely to have insight into the victim's trauma response.

Emergency room staff should test for and provide information on STDs and pregnancy. They will give her the option of the morning-after pill to avoid an unwanted pregnancy.

Medical assistance is an important option if a woman has been raped. A woman who does not want to go to the emergency room or urgent care should be urged to go to her family doctor as soon as possible so that she get the morning-after pill if she so chooses and receive testing for STDs.

Support Groups

Within your community may be a number of support groups. They can be found through universities, colleges, community colleges, high school counselors, all-women twelve-step groups, and hospitals. The support groups can include grief groups, AMAC (Adults Molested As Children), and rape survivor groups. Rape-crisis centers and domestic violence shelters often provide such support groups.

Printed and Electronic Resources

There are several books that can be useful for survivors. Two that I recommend are *I Never Called It Rape: The Ms. Report on Recognizing, Fighting, and Surviving Date and Acquaintance Rape* by Robin Warshaw, and *No Fairy Godmothers, No Magic Wands: The Healing Process after Rape* by Judy Katz (see bibliography for full citations).

For pastoral care providers, I recommend: *The Cry of Tamar: Violence against Women and the Church's Response* by Pamela Cooper-White (particularly the chapter on rape), *Intimate Betrayal: Understanding and Responding to the Trauma of Acquaintance Rape* by Vernon R. Wiehe and Ann L. Richards, and *Coping with Date Rape and Acquaintance Rape* by

Andrea Parrot. Also, Rebecca Voelkel-Haugen and Marie Fortune's *Sexual Abuse Prevention: A Course Study for Teenagers* is a workshop curriculum designed to help adolescents prevent and talk about sexual abuse.

For survivors and careproviders I recommend "Love: All That and More," a video series designed to inform adolescents and young adults about what makes for healthy relationships, how to understand relational abuse, and ways to develop relationships built on equality and mutual respect (see bibliography for full citation).

There are several organizations with websites that contain information for both survivors and care providers:

- Rape, Abuse, and Incest National Network (RAINN): http://www.rainn.org/counseling.html or 1-800-656-HOPE
- Institute on Domestic Violence in the African American Community: http://www.dvinstitute.org
- National Domestic Violence Hotline (contains all the 24-hour crisis phone numbers in the United States, listing them by states): http://www.feminist.org/911/crisis.html#hotline or 1-800-799-SAFE
- National Clearinghouse for Marital and Date Rape (for researchers, public educators, litigation advocates, and organizers): http://members.aol.com/ncmdr/
- The Center for the Prevention of Sexual and Domestic Violence: http://www.cpsdv.org
- The Interfaith Sexual Trauma Institute: http://www.csbsju.edu/isti/

6.

When Violence Is No Stranger

It was early in my ministry when a survivor of acquaintance rape first came to see me for help. At some level I realized that she was entrusting me with her very fragile soul. At the time, however, it felt less like an honor and more like a view into her own private hell. I knew that God was in the midst of her nightmare, giving her the courage and the power to wake up each day, but I was unclear about my place in that drama. In my years of work in pastoral care there have been issues that have turned my head, but none as much as acquaintance rape. I have not experienced the first-hand horrors known by survivors. I do, however, know anger at rapists, anger at slow legal processes, anger at abrupt law enforcement officials, and yes, even anger at survivors. And I have felt the shame that goes along with feeling ill-equipped to help. More than once, I have listened to a woman after she was raped and wanted to make either a swift difference or a sudden exit: all or nothing. The trauma of rape can do that to a caregiver. Of course, neither efficiency nor denial is a realistic goal for pastoral care.

When violence is no stranger, a woman can be raped by someone she knows, trusts, and loves. Such a brutal incongruity violates her physically, relationally, sexually, and incarnationally. Acquaintance rape has the power to shatter a woman's psycho-spiritual environment, destroying her ability to make sense of her world. She experiences this brokenness as betrayal, self-blame, desecration of the body, loss of normalcy, confusion about the violence, and loss of a redemptive community. Speaking the truth of rape starts with a woman's finding a safe-enough person who is willing and able to hear her sufferings. Know the truth and the truth shall set you free: it sounds like such a righteous endeavor. For survivors of acquaintance rape, however, knowing and speaking the truth is frightening and shame-filled. Much later in the survivor's healing process, knowing the truths about her violation can indeed set her free to live a fuller life. But as with other forms of trauma, freedom rarely is felt in the immediacy of the struggle to make sense of the shattering. Telling the truth is hard work when the truth shakes up the way a woman lives in the world.

In the midst of the suffering, there is salvific healing. Naming acquaintance rape as violence and asserting (and believing) that it is not the woman's fault are the starting point for healing. Support from friends, family, and professional caregivers can make a difference in whether she will experience severe long-term effects. Healing means attending to a new identity and orienting herself to a new understanding of her world. This reconstructive work happens as a women finds ways to make meaning after the rape, refuses to let evil have the final word, gets angry at the rapist and the injustice of the act, and reclaims her place in her community of friends and faith. These healing components are crucial to a woman as they help her turn from brokenness to hope.

When violence is no stranger, a pastoral caregiver is called to take off her or his shoes and gently accompany the woman over the sacred ground of her hard journey. In the name of God, we are called to stand with a survivor in her suffering, not because there is something valorous to learn from the violence or because suffering makes us stronger, but because where two or three are gathered, suffering can be overcome. Through God, our presence can make a positive difference in a survivor's healing.

Accompanying a woman through the storm of her feelings requires the caregiver to have patience, courage, and a firm conviction that God is on the survivor's side. It is not enough to "do no harm." Because a survivor can experience a profound betrayal of trust, working with a survivor means pushing beyond our own comfort zone and meeting her in her suffering. Practically speaking, this means believing in the face of disbelief, having patience in the face of shame and confusion, being an advocate without taking over, creating a safe space without requiring the survivor to feel safe, and telling the truth when we just don't know the answers. The majority of religious professionals are not medical experts, legal professionals, rape-crisis counselors, or even pastoral psychotherapists. Our gifts need not duplicate these important services. As members and leaders of faith communities, we are invited to join survivors as they look for ways to find and make embodied meaning in light of their faith and their larger communities. Informed pastoral care with a survivor of acquaintance rape creates the possibility of a safe-enough space for a woman to resanctify her body, replenish her soul, and reclaim her redemptive community.

When violence is no stranger, a community of faith is called to create a safe-enough place for a woman to tell her story and know that she is affirmed. Communities of faith can draw on their historical resources of scriptures, liturgies, prayers, and more to provide a much-needed balm. It's not easy for the church and other faith communities to talk about evil that is real, embodied, and sexualized. Acquaintance rape is difficult for people of faith because it is personal, intimate, and confusing. Working to understand acquaintance rape forces members of a community to admit that sometimes they can only believe what has enough tangible evidence to dispel all doubt. The nature of acquaintance rape means that there will always be doubt, both for survivors and communities. To be redemptive for survivors, communities must work to identify and move beyond these coping mechanisms of denial, repression, and dissociation from tough issues. Just as survivors must struggle with these defense or coping mechanisms so, too, must communities who desire to provide true sanctuary.

In a training session on legal rights of survivors of sexualized violence, a felony prosecutor from San Bernardino County, California, delivered a stinging indictment when she said, "[Sexualized violence] is the kind of violence that people in ivory towers don't want to deal with."[1] Addressing acquaintance rape is uncomfortable for religious professionals and all of us. As members of the body of Christ, we are called down from these towers of denial and fear to hear the good news of liberation for the oppressed. This liberation frees us from the power of evil to live redemptive and caring lives. To proclaim this good news of hope, we must first name our very brokenness. The hope of healing starts with naming our lamentations. Because violence is no stranger, the gospel empowers us to name the violence that oppresses, lament the doubt that shames, and reclaim the hope of a redemptive community.

Notes

1. Introduction

1. American Association of Pastoral Counselors, petition, presented to Hillary Rodham Clinton on behalf of heath care reform, American Association of Pastoral Counselors Conference, 1993, cited in Laura Delaplain, *Cutting a New Path: Helping Survivors of Childhood Domestic Trauma* (Cleveland: United Church Press, 1997), xv.

2. Judith Lewis Herman, *Trauma and Recovery* (New York: Basic Books, 1992), 61.

3. Dean G. Kilpatrick, Christine N. Edmunds, and Anne Seymour, *Rape in America: A Report to the Nation* (Arlington, Va.: National Victim Center, 1992), i.

4. Division of Adolescent and School Health, *Youth Risk Behavior Surveillance: National College Health Risk Behavior Survey – United States* (Washington, D.C.: National Center for Chronic Disease Prevention and Health Promotion, 1995).

5. Kilpatrick et al., *Rape in America*, 3.

6. Gail E. Wyatt, "The Sociocultural Context of African American and White American Women's Rape," *Journal of Social Issues* 48 (Spring 1992): 80.

7. Kilpatrick et al., *Rape in America*, 6, 14.

8. Patricia Tjaden and Nancy Thoennes, *Full Report of the Prevalence, Incidence, and Consequences of Violence against Women: Findings from the National Violence against Women Survey* (Washington, D.C.: National Institute of Justice, 2000), 4. The literature makes a clear distinction between sexual assault against a child and the violent use of sex against adults.

9. Patricia Searles and Ronald J. Berger, "The Current Status of Rape Reform Legislation: An Examination of State Statutes," *Women's Rights Law Reporter* 10 (1987): 41.

10. I draw on Toinette Eugene's definition of sexual abuse for these four areas. For more on this, see Toinette Eugene, "'Swing Low, Sweet Chariot!' A Womanist Ethical Response to Sexual Violence and Abuse," in *Violence against Women and Children: A Christian Theological Sourcebook,* ed. Carol J. Adams and Marie Fortune (New York: Continuum, 1995), 187.

11. Throughout this work I use the term *victim* to refer to women near the time of the rape and *survivor* to denote women who have moved beyond the immediacy of the trauma and have started the reorganizational phase of healing.

12. Sharon D. Parks, *The Critical Years: Young Adults and the Search for Meaning, Faith, and Commitment* (San Francisco: HarperSanFrancisco, 1986), 75.

13. Susan Estrich, *Real Rape* (Cambridge, Mass.: Harvard University Press, 1987), 4.

14. Mary Koss, Thomas Dinero, Cynthia Seibel, and Susan Cox, "Stranger and Acquaintance Rape: Are There Differences in the Victim's Experience?" *Psychology of Women Quarterly* 12 (1988): 20.

15. Anita Diamant, *The Red Tent* (New York: St. Martin's, 1997).

16. Pamela Cooper-White, *The Cry of Tamar: Violence against Women and the Church's Response* (Minneapolis: Fortress Press, 1995), 14.

17. Marie Fortune, *Sexual Violence: The Unmentionable Sin* (Cleveland: Pilgrim, 1983), 43.

18. Cooper-White, *Cry of Tamar,* 95. For the original work on the wounded healer, see Henri Nouwen, *The Wounded Healer: Ministry in Contemporary Society* (New York: Doubleday, 1979).

19. Herman, *Trauma and Recovery,* 140.

20. Cooper-White, *Cry of Tamar,* 196.

21. Marsha Foster-Boyd, "Womanist Care," paper presented at the American Academy of Religion, Chicago, Ill., November 17, 1995.

22. For more a feminist method of research, see Sandra Harding, "Introduction: Is There a Feminist Method?" in *Feminism and Methodology*, ed. Sandra Harding (Bloomington: Indiana University Press, 1987), 6.

2. Facts and Theories about Acquaintance Rape

1. Vernon R. Wiehe and Ann L. Richards, *Intimate Betrayal: Understanding and Responding to the Trauma of Acquaintance Rape* (Thousand Oaks, Calif.: Sage, 1995), 10–14.

2. In marital rapes, one in seven women had been raped one or more times by husbands or ex-husbands. As many as 46 percent of rapes, that is one out of every two rapes, are committed by fathers, stepfathers, husbands, ex-husbands, and other relatives (ibid., 14).

3. Federal Bureau of Investigation. "Forcible Rape." *Uniform Crime Reports,* Section II: Crime Index Offenses Reported, 1998 [February 28, 2000]. On-line: http://www.fbi.gov/ucr/98cius.htm.

4. "Sexual Assault Statistics," *Research and Advocacy Digest* 1 (February 1999): 10.

5. Patricia Tjaden and Nancy Thoennes, *Full Report of the Prevalence, Incidence, and Consequences of Violence against Women: Findings from the National Violence against Women Survey* (Washington, D.C.: National Institute of Justice, 2000), 46.

6. David Finkelhor, "Current Information on the Scope and Nature of Child Sexual Abuse," *The Future of Children* 4 no. 2 (1994): 46.

7. Mary Koss, Thomas Dinero, Cynthia Seibel, and Susan Cox, "Stranger and Acquaintance Rape: Are There Differences in the Victim's Experience?" *Psychology of Women Quarterly* 12 (1988): 13.

8. "Sexual Assault Statistics," 44.

9. Pamela Cooper-White, *The Cry of Tamar: Violence against Women and the Church's Response* (Minneapolis: Fortress Press, 1995), 85.

10. Frank Julian, "Date and Acquaintance Rape: The Legal Point of View: Part 1," *College Student Affairs Journal* 12 (Spring 1993): 6.

11. Audre Lorde, *Sister Outsider: Essays and Speeches* (Trumansburg, N.Y.: Crossing, 1984), 120.

12. William Ryan, *Blaming the Victim* (New York: Pantheon, 1971), 19.

13. Wiehe and Richards, *Intimate Betrayal,* 20.

14. Geraldo M. Gonzalez, "A Comparison of Alcohol Use and Alcohol-Related Problems among Caucasian, Black and Hispanic College Students," *NASPA Journal* 27 (1990): 334.

15. Bureau of Justice Statistics, *BJS Data Report* (Rockville, Md.: National Criminal Justice Reference Service/BJS Clearinghouse, 1986), 12.

16. Pauline Bart and Patricia O'Brien, *Stopping Rape: Successful Survival Strategies* (New York: Pergamon, 1985), 86.

17. Gail E. Wyatt, "The Sociocultural Context of African American and White American Women's Rape," *Journal of Social Issues* 48 (Spring 1992): 86.

18. Cooper-White, *Cry of Tamar*, 88.

19. Eileen O'Brien, "Black Women Additionally Victimized by Myths, Stereotypes: Scholars Say More Research Needed," *Black Issues in Higher Education* (December 7, 1989): 9.

20. Patricia Tjaden and Nancy Thoennes, "Extent, Nature, and Consequences of Intimate Partner Violence" (Washington, D.C.: National Institute of Justice, 2000), 53.

21. Wyatt, "Sociocultural Context," 78.

22. Angela Y. Davis, *Women, Race and Class* (New York: Random House, 1981), 175.

23. Darlene Clark Hine, "Rape and the Inner Lives of Black Women in the Middle West: Preliminary Thoughts on the Culture of Dissemblance," *Signs: Journal of Women in Culture and Society* 14 (1989): 912.

24. Davis, *Women, Race and Class,* 25.

25. Ibid., 7.

26. Ibid., 183.

27. Ibid.

28. Susan Brownmiller, *Against Our Will: Men, Women, and Rape* (New York: Simon and Schuster, 1975), 240.

29. Emilie M. Townes, *Womanist Justice, Womanist Hope* (Atlanta: Scholars, 1993), 138.

30. For in-depth critiques of Brownmiller and others, see Angela Y. Davis, "Rape, Racism, and the Capitalist Setting," *Black Scholar* 12 (November/December 1981): 39–45; idem, *Women, Race and Class,* 78.

31. Toinette Eugene, "'Swing Low, Sweet Chariot!' A Woman's Ethical Response to Sexual Violence and Abuse," in *Violence against Women and Children: A Christian Theological Sourcebook*, ed. Carol J. Adams and Marie Fortune (New York: Continuum, 1995), 187.

32. This leaves me wondering: When a woman's identity involves survival and resistance all the time, is it psychically safe to believe that

you have been violated when society and your community may deny it?

33. Wyatt, "Sociocultural Context," 80.

34. O'Brien, "Black Women," 9.

35. Anita P. Jackson and Susan J. Sears, "Implications of an Afrocentric Worldview in Reducing Stress for African American Women," *Journal of Counseling and Development* 71 (November/December 1992): 186.

36. Eileen O'Brien, "Date Rape: Hidden Epidemic Makes Campuses Unsafe for Women," *Black Issues in Higher Education* (December 7, 1989): 9.

37. N. Duncan Sinclair, *Horrific Traumata: A Pastoral Response to the Post-Traumatic Stress Disorder* (New York: Haworth Pastoral, 1993), 15.

38. Ruth E. Krall, *Rape's Power to Dismember Women's Lives: Personal Realities and Cultural Forms* (Ph.D. diss., School of Theology at Claremont, 1990; Ann Arbor, Mich.: UMI, 1990), 152.

39. Ann W. Burgess and Lynda L. Holmstrom, "Rape Trauma Syndrome," *American Journal of Psychiatry* 131 (September 1974): 981–85.

40. Ibid., 982.

41. In later works, Burgess and Holmstrom break this syndrome into three phases: the acute or impact stage, the recoil or pseudo-adjustment stage, and the integration or reorganization stage.

42. Burgess and Holmstrom, "Rape Trauma Syndrome," 982; Ann W. Burgess and Lynda L. Holmstrom, *Rape: Victims of Crisis* (Bowie, Md.: Brady, 1974), 40.

43. Burgess and Holmstrom do not comment on those who may dissociate from their feelings. I wonder if it is because this reaction occurs more commonly with a compounded reaction to a trauma, that is, a more severe response, indicating past trauma and suggesting the need for something other than a crisis therapeutic approach.

44. Ann W. Burgess and Lynda L. Holmstrom, "Crisis and Counseling Requests of Rape Victims," *Nursing Research* 23 (May 1974): 199.

45. In working with survivors, I find it helpful to avoid using terms such as *paranoia, phobia,* and *overly sensitive* or *hypersensitive* when referring to survivors' reactions to everyday living. Because survivors of rape can struggle with questioning every move they

made before the rape, and because they feel (and are made to feel) that their sensitivity to their surroundings borders on obsessive, I prefer to use the term *hyperalertness* when describing a survivor's constant attention to her environment. This can help the survivor reframe her own normal responses to her different or altered way of being in her environment.

46. Sharon L. McCombie asserts that anger is a relatively rare reaction during and immediately after the assault ("Characteristics of Rape Victims Seen in Crisis Intervention," *Smith College Studies in Social Work* 46 [1976]: 153).

47. Burgess and Holmstrom, "Rape Trauma Syndrome," 983. In this early study, Burgess and Holmstrom interviewed victims of stranger rape and what we now call acquaintance rape. In their findings they did not name different feelings experienced by survivors of different categories of rape. In my research, I found that fear was not the survivors' primary feeling following the rape but disbelief, numbness, disgust, and betrayal.

48. Marie Fortune, *Sexual Violence: The Unmentionable Sin* (Cleveland: Pilgrim, 1983), 148.

49. Roxane L. Silver and Camille B. Wortman, "Coping with Undesirable Life Events," in *Human Helplessness: Theory and Application*, ed. Judy Garber and Martin Seligman (New York: Academic, 1980), 300.

50. Ann W. Burgess and Lynda L. Holmstrom, "Rape Trauma Syndrome and Post Traumatic Stress Response," in *Rape and Sexual Assault: A Research Handbook*, ed. Ann W. Burgess (New York: Garland, 1985), 53–54.

51. Ann W. Burgess, "Rape Trauma Syndrome," *Behavioral Science and the Law* 1 (1983): 99.

52. Burgess and Holmstrom, "Crisis and Counseling," 200.

53. Burgess and Holmstrom, "Rape Trauma Syndrome," 983.

54. Ibid., 984.

55. Burgess and Holmstrom draw on the work of Sandor Rado, who saw this phenomenon in war victims. See Rado, "Pathodynamics and Treatment of Traumatic War Neuroses (Traumatophobia)," *Psychosomatic Medicine* 4 (1948): 362–68. Today we would call this post-traumatic stress disorder.

56. Burgess and Holmstrom, "Rape Trauma Syndrome," 985.

57. Burgess and Holmstrom, *Rape: Victims of Crisis,* 109.

58. Burgess and Holmstrom, "Rape Trauma Syndrome," 984.

59. Burgess and Holmstrom, *Rape: Victims of Crisis,* 48.

60. Robert Kastenbaum, "Is Death a Life Crisis? On the Confrontation with Death in Theory and Practice," in *Life-Span Developmental Psychology,* ed. Nancy Datan and Leon H. Ginsberg (New York: Academic, 1975), 37.

61. Silver and Wortman, "Coping with Undesirable Life Events," 307.

62. Ibid., 335.

63. Ibid., 281.

64. Burgess and Holmstrom, *Rape: Victims of Crisis,* 100.

65. Edward P. Wimberly, *Counseling African American Marriages and Families* (Louisville: Westminster John Knox, 1997), 13.

66. Ruth Krall uses the term *bodyself* to mean "the original core of being that cannot be contained or possessed." Ruth Krall, "Christian Ideology, Rape, and Women's Postrape Journeys to Healing," in *Peace Theology and Violence against Women,* ed. Elizabeth G. Yoder (Elkhart, Ind.: Institute of Mennonite Studies, 1992), 76.

67. Lenore E. A. Walker, *Abused Women and Survivor Therapy: A Practical Guide for the Psychotherapist* (Washington, D.C.: American Psychological Association, 1994), 26.

68. Harold Kaplan, Benjamin Sadock, and Jack Grebb, *Kaplan and Sadock's Synopsis of Psychiatry: Behavioral Sciences, Clinical Psychiatry,* 7th ed. (Baltimore: Williams and Wilkins, 1994), 606.

69. Edna B. Foa, Gail Steketee, and Barbara Olasov Rothbaum, "Behavioral/Cognitive Conceptualizations of Post-Traumatic Stress Disorder," *Behavior Therapy* 20 (1989): 155.

70. Judith Lewis Herman, *Trauma and Recovery* (New York: Basic Books, 1992), 28.

71. American Psychiatric Association, *Diagnostic and Statistical Manual of Mental Disorder* (Washington D.C.: American Psychiatric Association, 1952).

72. American Psychiatric Association, *Diagnostic and Statistical Manual of Mental Disorder: DSM-II* (Washington D.C.: American Psychiatric Association, 1968).

73. American Psychiatric Association, *Diagnostic and Statistical Manual of Mental Disorder:DSM-III,* 3rd ed. (Washington D.C.: American Psychiatric Association, 1980).

74. American Psychiatric Association, *Diagnostic and Statistical Manual of Mental Disorders: DSM-IV*, 4th ed. (Washington, D.C.: American Psychiatric Association, 1994), 424. In its current version, the DSM-IV has made some changes in the qualifiers first listed in the DSM-III and DSM-III-R. In the DSM-III and III-R it was understood that in order for an event to match the criteria for PTSD it had to be "outside the range of normal human experience." In the DSM-IV this was deleted because it was unreliable and inaccurate. This would be especially true in the case of forms of sexualized violence. Instead the DSM-IV requires that the person's response to the stressor involve intense fear, helplessness, or horror. The works of Lenore Walker and Judith Lewis Herman, from which I draw substantial information, are based on the DSM-III and III-R. No research has yet been published on rape and PTSD based on the DSM-IV criteria.

75. The DSM-IV notes that the symptomatology for children may have different manifestations.

76. PTSD differs from an adjustment disorder in that with adjustment disorders there is an abnormal emotional reaction to a normal lifecycle situational event. For more on this, see Walker, *Abused Women and Survivor Therapy*, 76.

77. Ibid., 35.

78. Sinclair, *Horrific Traumata*, 37.

79. Walker, *Abused Women and Survivor Therapy*, 36.

80. This is relevant to survivors of acquaintance rape because 41 percent of survivors say they expect to be raped again. Robin Warshaw, *I Never Called it Rape: The Ms. Report on Recognizing, Fighting, and Surviving Date and Acquaintance Rape* (New York: Harper & Row, 1988), 64.

81. Kaplan et al., *Kaplan and Sadock's Synopsis of Psychiatry*, 610.

82. American Psychiatric Association, *DSM-IV*, 429.

83. Barbara Olasov Rothbaum, Edna B. Foa, David S. Riggs, Tamera Murdock, and William Walsh, "A Prospective Examination of Post-Traumatic Stress Disorder in Rape Victims," *Journal of Traumatic Stress* 5 (1992): 470.

84. Dean G. Kilpatrick, Benjamin E. Saunders, Lois J. Vernon, Connie L. Best, and Judith M. Von, "Criminal Victimization: Lifetime Prevalence, Reporting to Police, and Psychological Impact," *Crime and Delinquency* 33 (October 1987): 484.

85. Fran H. Norris, "Epidemiology of Trauma: Frequency and Impact of Different Potentially Traumatic Events of Different Demographic Groups," *Journal of Consulting and Clinical Psychology* 60, no. 3 (1992): 409.

86. Edna B. Foa, Gail Steketee, and Barbara Olasov Rothbaum, "Behavioral/Cognitive Conceptualizations of Post-Traumatic Stress Disorder," *Behavior Therapy* 20 no. 2 (1989): 172.

87. Edna B. Foa, Barbara Olasov Rothbaum, and Gail Steketee, "Treatment of Rape Victims," *Journal of Interpersonal Violence* 8 (June 1993): 256.

88. Sinclair, *Horrific Traumata*, 37.

89. Walker, *Abused Women and Survivor Therapy*, 27.

90. Sinclair, *Horrific Traumata*, 37.

91. Koss and Harvey, *The Rape Victim*, 78.

92. American Psychiatric Association, *DSM-IV*, 683.

93. Ibid., 431.

94. Jeffrey Jay, "Walls for Wailing," *Common Ground* 12 (May/June 1994): 31.

95. Myung-Sook Lee, personal conversation, Claremont School of Theology, Claremont, Calif., July 27, 1998. For more on this discussion, see her forthcoming dissertation from the Claremont School of Theology.

96. Walker, *Abused Women and Survivor Therapy*, 30.

97. Ibid., 369, 373.

98. Ibid., 34.

3. The Survivors

1. Names and specific identifying information have been changed.

2. Memory loss is a common trauma-related symptom, as we detailed in chapter 2.

3. "Now Dinah the daughter of Leah, whom she had borne to Jacob, went out to visit the women of the region. When Shechem son of Hamor the Hivite, the prince of the region, saw her, he seized her and lay with her by force" (Gen. 34:1-2). The RSV adds, "and humbled her."

4. "David's son Absalom had a beautiful sister whose name was Tamar; and David's son Amnon fell in love with her. Amnon was so tormented that he made himself ill because of his sister Tamar, for she

was a virgin, and it seemed impossible to Amnon to do anything to her. But Amnon had a friend whose name was Jonadab, the son of David's brother Shimeah; and Jonadab was a very crafty man. He said to him, "O son of the king, why are you so haggard morning after morning? Will you not tell me?" Amnon said to him, "I love Tamar, my brother Absalom's sister." Jonadab said to him, "Lie down on your bed, and pretend to be ill; and when your father comes to see you, say to him, 'Let my sister Tamar come and give me something to eat, and prepare the food in my sight, so that I may see it, and eat it from her hand.'" So Amnon lay down, and pretended to be ill; and when the king came to see him, Amnon said to the king, "Pray let my sister Tamar come and make a couple of cakes in my sight, so that I may eat from her hand." Then David sent home to Tamar, saying, "Go to your brother Amnon's house, and prepare food for him." So Tamar went to her brother Amnon's house, where he was lying down. She took dough, and kneaded it, and made cakes in his sight, and baked the cakes. Then she took the pan and set them out before him, but he refused to eat. Amnon said, "Send out every one from me." So every one went out from him. Then Amnon said to Tamar, "Bring the food into the chamber, so that I may eat from your hand." So Tamar took the cakes she had made, and brought them into the chamber to Amnon her brother. But when she brought them near him to eat, he took hold of her, and said to her, "Come lie with me, my sister." She answered him, "No, my brother, do not force me; for such a thing is not done in Israel; do not do anything so vile! As for me, where could I carry my shame? And as for you, you would be as one of the scoundrels in Israel. Now therefore, I beg you, speak to the king; for he will not withhold me from you." But he would not listen to her; and being stronger than she, he forced her, and lay with her" (2 Sam. 13:1-14).

5. Melanie's confusion is particularly poignant in that it followed, by months, the very public trial of President Bill Clinton's sex scandal and his limiting the definition of sex to a penis ejaculating inside a vagina.

6. It is crucial for readers to note that it can be dangerous for a survivor to confront her perpetrator. If it ever happens, it must be initiated by the survivor and in a controlled environment where she is safe from further physical, communal, and psychospiritual harm.

4. A Pastoral Theological Framework

1. Eugene Kanin and Clifford Kirkpatrick wrote the first published articles on acquaintance rape in 1957. Eugene Kanin, "Male Aggression in Dating-Courtship Relations," *American Journal of Sociology* 63 (1957): 197–204; Clifford Kirkpatrick and Eugene Kanin, "Male Sex Aggression on a University Campus," *American Sociological Review* 22 (February 1957): 52–58.

2. Pamela Cooper-White, *The Cry of Tamar: Violence against Women and the Church's Response* (Minneapolis: Fortress Press, 1995), 98.

3. For more on these spiritual losses, see N. Duncan Sinclair, *Horrific Traumata: A Pastoral Response to the Post-Traumatic Stress Disorder* (New York: Haworth Pastoral, 1993), 43–69.

4. Herbert Ginsburg and Sylvia Opper, *Piaget's Theory of Intellectual Development: An Introduction* (Englewood Cliffs, N.J.: Prentice-Hall, 1969), 172.

5. Marie Fortune, *Sexual Violence: The Unmentionable Sin* (Cleveland: Pilgrim, 1983), 143.

6. Ronnie Janoff-Bulman, *Shattered Assumptions: Toward a New Psychology of Trauma* (New York: Free Press, 1992), 19.

7. Alice Miller, *Thou Shalt Not Be Aware: Society's Betrayal of the Child* (New York: Meridian, 1986), 95.

8. Fortune, *Sexual Violence*, 204; Mary D. Pellauer, "A Theological Perspective on Sexual Assault," in *Sexual Assault and Abuse: A Handbook for Clergy and Religious Professionals,* ed. Mary D. Pellauer, Barbara Chester, and Jane Boyajian (San Francisco: Harper & Row, 1987), 91.

9. Fortune, *Sexual Violence,* 204

10. Sinclair, *Horrific Traumata,* 72.

11. Fortune, *Sexual Violence,* 204.

12. Emilie Morgan, "Don't Call Me a Survivor," in *Listen Up: Voices from the Next Feminist Generation*, ed. Barbara Findlen (Seattle: Seal, 1995), 180.

13. Fortune, *Sexual Violence,* 34.

14. For a discussion on rape and the law, see Susan Estrich, *Real Rape* (Cambridge, Mass.: Harvard University Press, 1987); and Leslie Francis, ed., *Date Rape, Feminism, Philosophy, and the Law* (University Park: Pennsylvania State University Press, 1996).

15. Persuasion or seduction involves convincing a woman to act according to her own desires, though contrary to the duties imposed on her. Persuasion is not coercion, in that persuasion will take no for an answer. Coercion will not. Seduction means approaching someone who has both adequate information about sexuality *and* the power to consent or refuse. For more on this, see Lorenne Clark and Debra Lewis, *Rape: The Price of Coercive Sexuality* (Toronto: Women's Press, 1977), 175.

16. Fortune, *Sexual Violence,* 37.

17. In Christian marriage liturgies, the ring is often referred to as the "outward and visible sign of an inward and spiritual grace." See "A Service of Christian Marriage I," in *The United Methodist Book of Worship* (Nashville: Abingdon, 1992), 121.

18. I am indebted to the Rev. Marty Cash-Burliss, Chaplain at Mount Union College (Alliance, Ohio), for this term.

19. Jennifer Manlowe, *Faith Born of Seduction: Sexual Trauma, Body Image, and Religion* (New York: New York University Press, 1995), 67.

20. Fortune, *Sexual Violence,* 201.

21. Not her real name.

22. Celia J. Falicov, "Mexican Families," in *Ethnicity and Family Therapy,* ed. Monica McGoldrick, John Pearce, and Joseph Giordano (New York: Guilford, 1982), 134.

23. M. Shawn Copeland, "Wading through Many Sorrows: Toward a Theology of Suffering in Womanist Perspective," in *A Troubling in My Soul: Womanist Perspectives on Evil and Suffering,* ed. Emilie M. Townes (Maryknoll, N.Y.: Orbis, 1993), 124.

24. Ruth E. Krall, *Rape's Power to Dismember Women's Lives: Personal Realities and Cultural Forms* (Ph.D. diss., School of Theology at Claremont, 1990; Ann Arbor, Mich.: UMI, 1990), 38.

25. Judith Lewis Herman, *Trauma and Recovery* (New York: Basic Books, 1992), 51.

26. Fortune, *Sexual Violence,* 143.

27. Monique Savage, personal communication, 1997.

28. David Finkelhor, "Current Information on the Scope and Nature of Child Sexual Abuse," *The Future of Children* 4, no. 2 (1994), 41.

29. Herman, *Trauma and Recovery,* 178.

30. Kathleen M. Sands, *Escape from Paradise: Evil and Tragedy in Feminist Theology* (Minneapolis: Fortress Press, 1994), 65.

31. Fortune, *Sexual Violence,* 153.

32. Ibid., 194.

33. Ibid., 201.

34. Cooper-White, *The Cry of Tamar,* 97.

35. Marie Fortune, "Forgiveness: The Last Step," in *Abuse and Religion: When Praying Isn't Enough,* ed. Anne L. Horton and Judith A. Williamson (New York: Lexington, 1988), 218; John Patton, "Forgiveness, Lost Contracts, and Pastoral Theology," in *The Treasure of Earthen Vessels: Explorations in Theological Anthropology,* ed. Brian Childs and David Waanders (Louisville: Westminster John Knox, 1994), 206.

36. Pellauer, "Theological Perspective on Sexual Assault," 87.

5. Pastoral Counseling and Acquaintance Rape

1. Marie Fortune, *Sexual Violence: The Unmentionable Sin* (Cleveland: Pilgrim, 1983), 125.

2. Emma Justes, "Women," in *Clinical Handbook of Pastoral Counseling,* ed. Robert Wicks, Richard Parsons, and Donald Capps (New York: Paulist, 1985), 298.

3. Diane K. Beebe, "Emergency Management of the Adult Female Rape Victim," *American Family Physician* 43 (1991): 2041–46, cited in Lenore Walker, *Abused Woman and Survivor Therapy: A Practical Guide for the Psychotherapist* (Washington, D.C.: American Psychology Association, 1994), 29.

4. Mary Koss, W. J. Woodruff, and P. G. Koss, "Criminal Victimization among Primary Care Medical Patients: Incidence, Prevalence, and Physician Usage," *Behavioral Science and the Law* 9 (1991): 85–96.

5. Walker, *Abused Women and Survivor,* 29.

6. Kathleen Doheny, "What Date Rape Drugs Do," *Los Angeles Times*, October 8, 1996, E1. For more on this, see "Rohypnol 'Roofie' and Rape" (July 30, 1998), on-line: http://www.goaskalice.columbia.edu/0884.html.

6. When Violence Is No Stranger

1. Gail Solo, workshop on legal issues for a volunteer advocate's training session, Project SISTER, Sexual Assault Crisis and Prevention Services, Pomona, Calif., October 19, 1996.

Bibliography

Adams, Carol J., and Marie Fortune, eds. *Violence against Women and Children: A Christian Theological Sourcebook.* New York: Continuum, 1995.

American Psychiatric Association. *Diagnostic and Statistical Manual of Mental Disorders: DSM-IV.* 4th ed. Washington, D.C.: American Psychiatric Association, 1994.

Bohmer, Carol, and Andrea Parrot. *Sexual Assault on Campus: The Problem and the Solution.* New York: Lexington, 1993.

Brown, Joanne Carlson, and Carole R. Bohn, eds. *Christianity, Patriarchy, and Abuse: A Feminist Critique.* Cleveland: Pilgrim, 1989.

Brownmiller, Susan. *Against Our Will: Men, Women, and Rape.* New York: Simon & Schuster, 1975.

Buchwald, Emilie, Pamela R. Fletcher, and Martha Roth. *Transforming a Rape Culture.* Minneapolis: Milkweed Editions, 1993.

Burgess, Ann W., ed. *Rape and Sexual Assault: A Research Handbook.* New York: Garland, 1985.

Burt, Martha R. "Cultural Myths and Support for Rape." *Journal of Personality and Social Psychology* 38 (1980): 217–30.

Cooper-White, Pamela. *The Cry of Tamar: Violence against Women and the Church's Response.* Minneapolis: Fortress Press, 1995.

———. "Opening the Eyes: Understanding the Impact of Trauma on Development." In *In Her Own Time: Women and Developmental Issues in Pastoral Care,* ed. Jeanne Stevenson Moessner, 87–101. Minneapolis: Fortress Press, 2000.

Cromwell, Nancy A., and Ann W. Burgess, eds. *Understanding Violence against Women*. Washington, D.C.: National Academy Press, 1996.

Davis, Angela Y. "Rape, Racism, and the Capitalist Setting." *Black Scholar* 12 (November/December 1981): 39–45.

————. *Women, Race and Class*. New York: Random House, 1981.

Delaplain, Laura. *Cutting a New Path: Helping Survivors of Childhood Domestic Trauma*. Cleveland: United Church Press, 1997.

Diamant, Anita. *The Red Tent*. New York: St. Martin's, 1997.

Division of Adolescent and School Health. *Youth Risk Behavior Surveillance: National College Health Risk Behavior Survey—United States*. Washington, D.C.: National Center for Chronic Disease Prevention and Health Promotion, 1995.

Doheny, Kathleen. "What the Date Rape Drugs Do." *Lost Angeles Times*, October 8, 1996, E1.

Estrich, Susan. *Real Rape*. Cambridge, Mass.: Harvard University Press, 1987.

Eugene, Toinette, and James Poling. *Balm for Gilead: Pastoral Care for African American Families Experiencing Abuse*. Nashville: Abingdon, 1998.

Federal Bureau of Investigation. "Forcible Rape." *Uniform Crime Reports,* Section II: Crime Index Offenses Reported. 1998 [February 28, 2000]. On-line: http://www.fbi.gov/ucr/98cius.htm.

Fortune, Marie. *Sexual Violence: The Unmentionable Sin*. Cleveland: Pilgrim, 1983.

Francis, Leslie, ed. *Date Rape, Feminism, Philosophy, and the Law*. University Park: Pennsylvania State University Press, 1996.

Groth, A. Nicholas. *Men Who Rape: The Psychology of the Offender*. New York: Plenum, 1979.

Herman, Judith Lewis. *Trauma and Recovery*. New York: Basic Books, 1992.

Hine, Darlene Clark. "Rape and the Inner Lives of Black Women in the Middle West: Preliminary Thoughts on the Culture of Dissemblance." *Signs: Journal of Women in Culture and Society* 14 (1989): 912–20.

Horton, Anne L., and Judith A. Williamson, eds. *Abuse and Religion: When Praying Isn't Enough*. New York: Lexington, 1988.

Janoff-Bulman, Ronnie. *Shattered Assumptions: Toward a New Psychology of Trauma*. New York: Free Press, 1992.

Jay, Jeffrey. "Walls for Wailing." *Common Ground* 12 (May/June 1994): 30–35.

Julian, Frank H. "Date and Acquaintance Rape: The Legal Point of View: Part 1." *College Student Affairs Journal* 12 (Spring 1993): 3–10.

———. "Date and Acquaintance Rape: The Legal Point of View: Part 2." *College Student Affairs Journal* 12 (Spring 1993): 11–17.

Katz, Judy. *No Fairy Godmothers, No Magic Wands: The Healing Process after Rape*. Saratoga, Calif.: R and E, 1984.

Kilpatrick, Dean G., Christine N. Edmunds, and Anne Seymour. *Rape in America: A Report to the Nation*. Arlington, Va.: National Victim Center, 1992.

Koss, Mary, Thomas Dinero, Cynthia Seibel, and Susan Cox. "Stranger and Acquaintance Rape: Are There Differences in the Victim's Experience?" *Psychology of Women Quarterly* 12 (1988): 1–24.

Koss, Mary, Christine Gidycz, and Nancy Wisniewski. "The Scope of Rape: Incidence and Prevalence of Sexual Aggression and Victimization in a National Sample of Higher Education Students." *Journal of Consulting and Clinical Psychology* 55 (1987): 162–70.

Koss, Mary P., and Mary R. Harvey. *The Rape Victim: Clinical and Community Interventions*. 2nd ed. Newbury Park, Calif.: Sage, 1991.

Krall, Ruth E. *Rape's Power to Dismember Women's Lives: Personal Realities and Cultural Forms*. Ph.D. diss., School of Theology at Claremont, 1990; Ann Arbor, Mich.: UMI, 1990.

———. "Christian Ideology, Rape, and Women's Postrape Journeys to Healing." In *Peace Theology and Violence against Women,* ed. Elizabeth G. Yoder, 73–85. Elkhart, Ind.: Institute of Mennonite Studies, 1992.

Levy, Barrie, ed. Dating Violence: Young Women in Danger. Seattle: Seal, 1998.

"Love: All That and More." A three-video series created and distributed by the Center for the Prevention of Sexual and Domestic Violence, Seattle, Wa.; http://www.cpsdv.org.

Manlowe, Jennifer. *Faith Born of Seduction: Sexual Trauma, Body Image, and Religion*. New York: New York University Press, 1995.

McClure, John, and Nancy Ramsay, eds. *Telling the Truth: Preaching about Sexual and Domestic Violence.* Cleveland: Pilgrim, 1998.

Michigan Department of Community Health. *Watch Out for Rape Drugs.* Lansing: Michigan Women's Commission, 2002.

Neuger, Christie Cozad. *Counseling Women: A Narrative, Pastoral Approach.* Minneapolis: Fortress Press, 2001.

———. "Narratives of Harm: Setting the Developmental Context for Intimate Violence." In *In Her Own Time: Women and Developmental Issues in Pastoral Care,* ed. Jeanne Stevenson Moessner, 65–86. Minneapolis: Fortress Press, 2000.

O'Brien, Eileen. "Black Women Additionally Victimized by Myths, Stereotypes: Scholars Say More Research Needed." *Black Issues in Higher Education* (December 7, 1989): 8–9.

———. "Date Rape: Hidden Epidemic Makes Campuses Unsafe for Women." *Black Issues in Higher Education* (December 7, 1989): 6–10.

Parrot, Andrea, and Laurie Bechhofer, eds. *Acquaintance Rape: The Hidden Crime.* New York: Wiley and Sons, 1991.

Pellauer, Mary D., Barbara Chester, and Jane Boyajian, eds. *Sexual Assault and Abuse: A Handbook for Clergy and Religious Professionals.* San Francisco: Harper & Row, 1987.

Piercy, Marge. "Rape Poem." In *Circles on the Water: Selected Poems of Marge Piercy*. New York: Knopf, 1982.

Ramsay, Nancy. "Sexual Abuse and Shame: The Travail of Recovery." In *Women in Travail and Transition: A New Pastoral Care,* eds. Maxine Glaz and Jeanne Stevenson Moessner, 109–25. Minneapolis: Fortress Press, 1991.

"Sexual Assault Statistics." *Research and Advocacy Digest* 1 (February 1999).

Sinclair, N. Duncan. *Horrific Traumata: A Pastoral Response to the Post-Traumatic Stress Disorder*. New York: Haworth Pastoral, 1993.

Stinson-Wesley, S. Amelia. "Daughters of Tamar: Pastoral Care for Survivors of Rape." In *Through the Eyes of Women: Insights for Pastoral Care,* ed. Jeanne Stevenson Moessner, 222–39. Minneapolis: Fortress Press, 1996.

Tjaden, Patricia, and Nancy Thoennes. *Extent, Nature, and Consequences of Intimate Partner Violence*. Washington, D.C.: National Institute of Justice, 2000.

———. *Full Report of the Prevalence, Incidence, and Consequences of Violence against Women: Findings from the National Violence against Women Survey*. Washington, D.C.: National Institute of Justice, 2000.

Townes, Emilie M., ed. *A Troubling in My Soul: Womanist Perspectives on Evil and Suffering*. Maryknoll, N.Y.: Orbis, 1993.

Voelkel-Haugen, Rebecca, and Marie Fortune. *Sexual Abuse Prevention: A Course of Study for Teenagers*. Rev. ed. Cleveland: United Church Press, 1996.

Walker, Lenore E. A. *Abused Women and Survivor Therapy: A Practical Guide for the Psychotherapist*. Washington, D.C.: American Psychological Association, 1994.

Warshaw, Robin. *I Never Called It Rape: The Ms. Report on Recognizing, Fighting, and Surviving Date and Acquaintance Rape*. New York: Harper & Row, 1988.

West, Traci C. *Wounds of the Spirit: Black Women, Violence, and Resistance Ethics*. New York: New York University Press, 1999.

Wiehe, Vernon R., and Ann L. Richards. *Intimate Betrayal: Understanding and Responding to the Trauma of Acquaintance Rape*. Thousand Oaks, Calif.: Sage, 1995.

Wyatt, Gail E. "The Sociocultural Context of African American and White American Women's Rape." *Journal of Social Issues* 48 (Spring 1992): 77–91.

Wyatt, Gail E., Cindy M. Notgrass, and Michael Newcomb. "Internal and External Mediators of Women's Rape Experiences." *Psychology of Women Quarterly* 14 (1990): 153–76.

Index

Genesis 34:1-2, 8.
See also Dinah
Genesis 32:24-30,
105–6. *See also*
Jacob
John 1:5, 125
Judges 19, 21
Luke 10:29-37, 8–9,
130. *See also* Good
Samaritan
Psalm 55:12-14, 1
black women: *See*
African American
women
blame, 6, 82–83
blaming the victim,
111, 149
lack of, 134
See also self-blame
bodily integrity, 4, 100
body, 29, 100
cleansing of, 116
desecration of the,
101, 111–13, 116
sacredness, 116
scene of crime,
111–13, 116
violation of, 126
bodyself, 40n.66
boys: *See* male sur-
vivors
Brownmiller, Susan,
25
Burgess, Ann, 28–41,
29n.41

caregiver, 9. *See also*
religious profes-
sional

careprovider, 36. *See
also* religious pro-
fessional
Cash-Burliss, Marty,
114n.18
Center for the Pre-
vention of Sexual
and Domestic Vio-
lence, 152, 154,
176
chastity, 115
child abuse, 15
children, 44, 45, 46
child sexual abuse
syndrome, 54
Christian marriage
liturgy, 113n.17
Christian tradition, 7,
7–10, 100
church, 9. *See also*
faith community
clergy, 50. *See also*
religious profes-
sional
Clinton, Bill, 80n.5
coercion, 110 n.15
cognitive dissonance,
2, 47, 106
common sense, 40.
See also intuition
communal ties, loss
of, 120–24
community
agency, 74, 150–52
endangering of, 75
as holding environ-
ment, 128–29
loss of, 93, 101
protection of, 120

redemptive power
of, 128–29
safety of, 66
support, 95
trust of, 121
confidentiality, 134
consensual questions,
110–11
consensual sex, 6, 35,
44, 57, 76. *See also*
consent
consent, 4, 7, 20, 78,
82–83, 86, 105–6,
108–11
age of, 11
definition of,
109–10
inability to give, 36
lack of, 11, 15, 79,
80, 82, 102,
110n.15
principle of, 110
as psychospiritual
issue, 7
control, 67, 69, 91
lack of, 90–92
loss of, 46
Cooper-White,
Pamela, 8, 9, 10,
154
Copeland, M. Shawn,
115
coping mechanisms,
29, 45, 51, 157
countertransference,
48
court, 28, 59, 145-48
crime scene, 111–13
conviction rates, 20

presence of, 103, 155, 156
role in suffering, 104
and trauma, 40
See also Incarnate Spirit of God
golden rule, 131. See also Good Samaritan
Good Samaritan, 8–9, 129–31. See also biblical resources: Luke 10:29-37
grief, 70–72, 127
loss of normalcy, 33, 92
loss of routine, 33
pathological, 144
guilt, 3, 15, 51, 105, 109, 137
gynecological exam, 37

Herman, Judith, 2, 42n.74, 117, 122
HIV, 147, 151
holding environment, 7, 100
Holmstrom, Lynda, 28–41nn.39, 41, 44
homeostasis, 100
hope, 46, 121
loss of, 100
hospital chaplain, 11, 39
hotline, 151
humiliation, 4, 31, 113–16, 147
hyperalertness, 30, 30n.45, 48, 136

identity, 5
embodied understanding of, 6
victim, 9
woman, 118
illusion of invulnerability, 102–3
Incarnate Spirit of God, 4, 100
incarnation, 155
incarnational violence, 4
insanity, fear of, 44, 51, 135
intergenerational trauma, 22, 27
intimacy, 5
loss of, 100
intoxication, 4. See also alcohol
intrusive thoughts, 31, 53
intuition, 32, 101, 117, 123, 131, 136
isolation, 46, 93

Jacob, 105. See also biblical resources: Genesis 32:24-30
Janoff-Bulman, Ronnie, 102–3
Jay, Jeffrey, 52–53
Judaism, 21, 52–53, 151, 152
Justes, Emma, 141
justice, 7, 8, 145, 150
just-world theory, 102–3

Kanin, Eugene, 99n.1

Katz, Judy, 153
Kirkpatrick, Clifford, 99n.1
Korean women, 53
Krall, Ruth, 40n.66, 117

lament, 103, 104, 157
Latin communities, 115
law enforcement, 3,19, 45. See also police
Lee, Myung-Sook, 53
legal system, 6, 11, 152
listening, 74, 85, 97, 133, 140
liturgical resources, 140, 149–50. See also biblical resources
loneliness, 53
Lorde, Audre, 18
lynching, 23–25

making meaning: See meaning-making
male survivors, 15, 36
malingering, 45, 52
marital rape, 11, 14n.2, 154
marriage, 46
Mary the temple prostitute, 108
McCombie, Sharon L., 31n.46
meaning, loss of, 100
meaning-making, 7, 39, 40, 99, 121–24

rape trauma syndrome (RTS), 28–41
compound reactions, 29, 30n.43, 35
definition, 29
history, 28–29
limitations of, 38
religious professionals and, 33, 38, 39
silent reactions, 29
rape
FBI definition of, 36, 80
law and, 110n.14
rapist: *See* perpetrator
real rape, 14, 25, 80, 106–8, 129–30
reconciliation, 127
Red Tent, The, 8
referrals, 2, 12, 36, 73, 139–40, 150, 150–54
regression, 35
religious education, 8
religious professional, 2, 7, 9, 10, 13, 14, 38, 39
accessibility, 129, 138–39
anger by, 105, 141, 155
boundary violations, 141
burnout, 10
consensual questions and, 111
countertransference, 143
effectiveness, 10

emergency rooms and, 146–47
empathy, 134, 140–43, 144
limitations of, 73, 138–42
male, 135, 143–44
mental health professionals and, 138
non-anxious presence, 134, 140–41
perceptions of, 138–39
perpetrator and, 145
role with family and friends, 149
safe space and, 141, 144
self-disclosure, 135
trauma of, 10
vicarious trauma, 143
women, 86, 135
religious resources, 21, 139, 142–43, 157. *See also* liturgical resources
reporting, 2, 3, 5, 88, 90
African American women, 25, 26
damage to community, 26
fear related to, 15
as healing, 20, 60
legal authorities, 15, 20, 58, 95, 135
public reaction, 26
rates of, 22

repression, 157
research methodology, 84
resistance, 10, 25n.32, 115, 117. *See also* womanist theology
retaliation, 97, 126. *See also* revenge
revenge, 24, 31, 69–70, 126
Richards, Ann L., 154
rituals, 144. *See also* religious resources
Roman Catholicism, 115

safe space, 111, 129, 134, 157
safety, 6, 7, 14, 15, 31, 33, 41, 45, 48, 49, 103, 119, 120, 131, 135, 136
assessment of, 133–34
psychospiritual, 102
Samaritan: *See* Good Samaritan
Sands, Kathleen, 122
sass, 115
Savage, Monique, 118
scene of the crime: *See* crime scene
secondary trauma: *See* vicarious trauma
secret, 64, 104, 117, 120, 148
seduction, 110n.15
self-acceptance, 83
self-blame, 3, 6, 18,